GROWING IN THE FAITH

BEING A DISCIPLE OF CHRIST

HAROLD BAYLEY

PAGE PUBLISHING
Conneaut Lake, PA

First originally published by Page Publishing 2024

ISBN 979-8-89315-953-0 (pbk)
ISBN 979-8-89315-969-1 (digital)

Printed in the United States of America

PROLOGUE

The purpose of this book has two main emphases. First, it is designed to help you grow in your faith and knowledge of the Lord Jesus Christ. This is the process known as sanctification. It is to help you overcome sin in your life and live a full rich life that is pleasing to the Lord. Second, it has a strong emphasis on biblical truth. There appears to be many false ideas being promoted among Christians in America today. Those false ideas have negative consequences in one's relationship with the Lord, and therefore, we should be aware of them so that we can escape the snare of the devil (1 Timothy 3:7).

Colossians 2:6–7 highlights the first emphasis: "So then, just as you received Christ Jesus as Lord, continue to live in him, rooted and built up in him, strengthened in the faith as you were taught, and overflowing with thankfulness" (NIV).

Acts 17:11 highlights the second emphasis: "Now these Jews were more noble than those in Thessalonica; they received the word with all eagerness, examining the Scriptures daily to see if these things were so" (ESV).

If you are looking for a book written by a well-known author, teacher, or preacher with a seminary degree and perhaps even a PhD, you are looking in the wrong place. If you are looking for a book that supports or adheres to one of the "isms," such as Calvinism, Arminianism, dispensationalism, determinism, preterism, Pelagianism, or any other "ism," again you are looking in the wrong place. It is my opinion that all systems of theology that are written or created by man will fall short of biblical truth in some way. It seems to me that most, if not all, have errors when it comes to particular doctrines in scripture. What you will find in this book is a lifelong journey of learning the Word of God, primarily from studying the scriptures. I have memorized several books of the New Testament and have taught classes at church. Although I have read many books by various authors and have consulted commentaries and the like, my primary focus has always been, "What does scripture say?"

The Bible quotations throughout this course are taken primarily from the English Standard Version of the Bible. Other quotations are from the 1984 edition of the New International Version and are so noted. Feel free to compare translations to get a fuller understanding of the verses covered. No single translation is a perfect duplication of the original texts.

SALVATION (PART 1)

In the beginning, God created the heavens and the earth and everything in them. Of all life that he created on earth, mankind was his highest creation. He created male and female, placed them in a garden, and enjoyed fellowship with them. When Adam and Eve disobeyed God's command to not eat of the tree of the knowledge of good and evil, they broke their fellowship with God and were driven from the garden. They had fallen into sin and became in need of salvation to restore the fellowship they once enjoyed. Furthermore, all mankind now inherits the same sin nature that Adam and Eve now had. Consequently, we are all in need of salvation from sin. God is working through all human history to deal with the issue of sin. At the end of the ages, he will have redeemed a people that are his very own and sin will be a thing of the past. Until that time, sin is the central issue that needs to be dealt with.

The bible speaks a lot about salvation. But what exactly is salvation, what are we saved from, and how does one attain it? Salvation is a concept simple enough for a child to understand and yet complex enough that there has been great debate down through the centuries concerning exactly what is involved in being saved. These lessons will help us understand what salvation is and how we are to become saved. They are also designed to help you become mature in your salvation; in other words, they will help you overcome sin in your life, among other things. If you are not yet in a saving relationship to Jesus Christ, or if you are not sure whether you are saved, carefully consider this lesson. If you are not yet saved, the rest of this course beyond lesson two will not be of much use to you. Thus, there is not much point in learning how to *be* a disciple of Christ until you *are* a disciple. Once you are initially saved, God's Holy Spirit will help you to apply the lessons in this course on discipleship.

When I stated, "If you are not yet in a saving relationship to Jesus Christ, or if you are not sure whether you are saved," I was referring to the initial act of salvation. There is a moment in time in which each person must come to faith in Christ. We will explore how that comes about. However, salvation is not just something that happens in a moment of time. It is an ongoing process that culminates in receiving a new imperishable body. It is critically important that we understand this concept. If we do, it will keep us from much doctrinal error that can do much damage to our spiritual well-being.

I am under the impression that the vast majority of Christians in America today do not understand that salvation is a continuing experience that culminates in the putting off of our perishable body and putting on an imperishable one. Here is how the Apostle Paul put it in a letter to the Corinthians, "For this perishable body must put on the imperishable, and this mortal body must put on immortality. When the perishable puts on the imperishable, and the mortal puts on immortality, then shall come to pass the saying that is written: "Death is swallowed up in victory" (1 Corinthians 15:53–54)

When we receive our imperishable body, we will have reached the culmination of the salvation process and neither sin nor death will ever affect us again.

Let's begin our study.

1. Read Matthew 25:31–46. According to verse 46, what are the two destinations of all mankind?

    a. _________________________________

    b. _________________________________

Notice that purgatory is not an option in this passage. Hebrews 9:27–28 helps in clarifying that once you die, you will face judgement: "And just as it is appointed for man to die once, and after that comes judgment, so Christ, having been offered once to bear the sins of many, will appear a second time, not to deal with sin but to save those who are eagerly waiting for him."

The Hebrews passage illustrates that once you die, then comes judgement, not purgatory, and upon being judged, you will either go to eternal life or eternal punishment. Your fate is sealed upon your death.

Jesus told a story about a rich man and Lazarus in Luke 16:19–31. Both died and Lazarus was taken to paradise (Abraham's bosom) and the rich man found himself in the torment of Hades (hell). The rich man asked Abraham to send Lazarus to cool his tongue with a little water but was told that no one could cross over from one side to the other. This story also illustrates that there is no purgatory. When the rich man and Lazarus both died, one went to eternal torment and the other went to paradise.

2. According to Romans 3:23, what is man's basic problem?
    ____

3. According to Romans 6:23, the wages of sin is __________ but the gift of God is _______________________________

4. According to Acts 4:8–12, where is salvation found?
    ____

5. Who is Jesus? Mark 1:1 _______________________________

This Jesus of whom salvation is found was God incarnate (John 1:1,14). Jesus was born of the virgin Mary (Luke 1:30–34). He lived a sinless life (1 John 3:5) and willingly died for us to atone for our sins and not only for ours, but also for the sins of the entire world (1 John 2:2) and then rose from the dead (Romans 1:1–4) and is alive forevermore. Having paid the penalty for sin, he has made salvation available to everyone.

It is important to understand what is meant by Jesus's atoning or making atonement for our sins. Atonement does not mean he forgave the sins of the world but rather that he made payment for the sins of the world. He paid the penalty for us so that we could be forgiven. He shed his blood so that our sins could be forgiven for his blood was shed to satisfy God's judgement on sin. It is when we believe and trust in Jesus Christ and what he did for us by dying on the cross that we can be forgiven.

According to Acts 4:12, since salvation only comes through Christ, what must we do to be saved? There are many passages that speak of salvation, but it boils down to two main principles. Consider the following passages.

6. What did the apostle Paul declare to both Jew and Gentile in Acts 20:21? ____________________________

   ____

   In Acts 26:14–18, Paul recounts the heavenly vision he received from Jesus Christ himself.

From this vision, Paul took the message of salvation to both Jew and Gentile.

7. What did the apostle Paul declare to both Jew and Gentile in Acts 26:19–20 as a result of the vision he received in Acts 26:14–18? ____________________________

8. What did Peter command as found in Acts 3:19? ________

   ____

9. What did John the Baptist preach in Mark 1:4? ________

   ____

10. When Jesus began his ministry, what did he preach in Mark 1:14–15? ____________________________

    ____

11. When Jesus sent the 12 disciples out, what did they preach according to Mark 6:7–12? ____________________________

    ____

12. In Acts 17:30, what did Paul tell the men of Athens concerning what God commands all people to do? _______________

We see that John the Baptist, Paul, Peter, the other disciples, and Jesus all preached that people should repent. Therefore, it is important to understand what is involved in repentance.

W. E. Vine's Greek Expository Dictionary of New Testament Words defines repent as: "to change one's mind or purpose, always, in the NT, involving a change for the better, an amendment, and always, except in Luke 17:3–4, of repentance from sin."[1]

There are some in Christian circles today that state that to repent only means a change of mind, thus robbing it of its full meaning. If you are headed to hell and only change your mind and not your direction, you will still be headed to hell. Repentance includes a change of mind as well as a change in direction or behavior. It is a repentance from sin. That is why the Apostle Paul instructs us in Acts 26:20 to perform deeds in keeping with our repentance. The verse from 2 Timothy 2:19 sums up what it means to repent. It says, "But God's firm foundation stands, bearing this seal: 'The Lord knows those who are his,'" and, "Let everyone who names the name of the Lord depart from iniquity." Departing from iniquity is what repentance is all about.

There are even some that declare that repentance is not necessary for salvation. Yet we see in Acts 2:38 that repentance brings the gift of the Holy Spirit, and it is the Holy Spirit that seals us. (Ephesians 1:13) Also, Jesus states that repentance for the forgiveness of sins should be preached in his name to all nations (Luke 24:47). We also saw above in question 8 that Acts 3:19 teaches repentance results in the blotting out or forgiveness of our sins. We saw earlier that sin is man's basic problem and that sin results in death (eternal death as opposed to eternal life which is the gift of God). Repentance

---

[1] W. E. Vine, *An Expository Dictionary Of New Testament Words: With Their Precise Meanings For English Readers*, vol. 3, p. 280 (Nashville, Tennessee: T. Nelson Publishers, 1985).

is what brings the forgiveness of our sins through the atonement provided by Jesus.

It should be noted that to repent of your sins does not mean you will never commit them again. What it does mean is that you will dedicate yourself to overcoming sin in your life with the help of God's Holy Spirit. This is the process of sanctification which we will cover in lesson 4.

Though repentance is necessary to receive the Holy Spirit and the forgiveness of sins, there is a second item involved in salvation.

13. What is the common theme in each of the following salvation passages?
    a.   John 3:16 _______________________________________
    b.   John 1:12–13 ____________________________________
    c.   Romans 10:9–10 __________________________________
    d.   Acts 16:31 _______________________________________

In Romans 10:9, Paul says we are to believe in our heart. This makes a distinction between mentally believing something to be true in our mind versus acting upon what you believe. We call this a head knowledge versus a heart knowledge.

In Romans 10:9, *believe* is the Greek word *pisteuo.* James 2:19 says, "You believe that there is one God. Good! Even the demons believe that—and shudder" (NIV). The demons are even said to believe, which is also the same Greek word, *pisteuo.* James goes on to show that just head knowledge, as the demons have, is not the kind of faith needed to believe in Christ Jesus. The word *believe* is an action verb and the word *faith* is a noun. To believe (verb) in Christ is the same as having faith (noun) in Christ. More of what James has to say will be discussed later.

In each of the preceding four passages, believe, is the Greek word *pisteuo. Pistis* is the Greek word for faith.

14. What do the following two passages say about faith?
    a.   Romans 4:9 ______________________________________
    b.   Ephesians 2:8 ____________________________________

Ephesians 2:8 introduces an important concept in salvation. It mentions that we are saved by God's grace. God's grace is unmerited. In other words, we cannot earn it by anything we do. It is also God's assistance in enabling us to come to salvation. He draws us and enables us to choose to receive Christ and believe in his name. He does not force us or choose for us but enables us. It is also God's grace that helps us in the process of progressive sanctification. We will also learn more about that later. Suffice it to say that without God's grace, we would be hopelessly lost.

15. According to Romans 5:2, how do we access God's grace? ____

16. Who does God give his grace to according to James 4:6? ____

Have you ever heard of being born again? Scripture defines what being born again is.

17. In John 3:3, what did Jesus say we need to do so that we could see the kingdom of God? ______________________
18. In John 3:5, what did Jesus say we need to do so that we could enter the kingdom of God? ______________________

Obviously, one cannot enter again into their mother's womb to be born again. What Jesus is referring to is a spiritual birth in contrast to a physical birth. John 1:12–13 clarifies this for us: "But to all who did receive him, who believed in his name, he gave the right to become children of God, who were born, not of blood nor of the will of the flesh nor of the will of man, but of God."

We see that receiving Christ and believing in his name gives us the right to become a child of God. In verse 13, it points out that becoming a child of God, or being born of God, is not brought about by human activity but rather it is brought about by God. This is a spiritual birth through receiving God's Holy Spirit. We are all born physically, but only those who experience a spiritual birth (born again or born of God) will inherit the kingdom of God. As verse 12 points out, this spiritual birth is a result of receiving and believing in Jesus Christ.

It is very important to understand the order of events in John 1:12–13. When you receive Christ and believe in his name, it is then that you have the right to *become* a child of God. Your faith is an important part of your salvation. There are those that actually teach that God saves you first and then gives you faith in Christ. This is backward to being born again as presented by John. More on this will be discussed in lesson 6 where I briefly discuss some of the teachings of John Calvin.

The Parable of the Sower

Read the parable found in Luke 8:4–8 and its interpretation in Luke 8:11–15.

19. What four places did the seed fall on?
    a. ____
    b. ____
    c. ____
    d. ____

When you heard the Word of God (the seed), what kind of ground did it fall on in your life? We know from verse 12 that you couldn't come to Christ had the seed fallen along the path because the devil takes the seed away so that you may not believe and be saved. So the question is, what kind of ground did the seed fall on in your life when it brought you to faith in Christ? Was it on the rocks, among the thorns, or on good soil? This may be a hard question to answer as we do not always know what is in our own heart. "The heart is deceitful above all things, and desperately sick; who can understand it?" (Jeremiah 17:9). However, it is important to know what soil is in your heart because the seed that fell on the rocks and the seed that fell among the thorns did not bear mature fruit. Those with that kind of soil fall away. It is only the one with good soil that produces fruit.

The seed that fell on the rocks resulted in that person falling away when their faith was tested.

20. Why is this a serious matter according to Hebrews 6:4–6?

____

____

When a time of testing comes, you have two choices. You can fall away from the faith, as those did whose seed fell among the rocks, or you can persevere through the trial.

21. How should you respond to trials as found in James 1:2–4, that will not only keep you from falling away, but will help you to grow stronger in your faith? _______________

____

22. What is the purpose of trials in the believers' life according to 1 Peter 1:6–7? _______________

____

23. In 2 Peter 1:5–10, what would be the remedy to keep you from falling or stumbling? _______________

____

The seed that fell among the thorns did not mature because of life's worries (or cares) and the riches and pleasures of this world.

24. How can you overcome the worries of this world according to Philippians 4:4–7? _______________

____

25. How can you overcome the worries of this world according to 1 Peter 5:7? _______________

____

26. How can you overcome the riches and pleasures of life so that they do not choke the Word according to 1 John 2:15–17? _______________

____

27. In your life, is the focus mainly on seeking pleasure or on the kingdom of God and helping the kingdom of God become a reality on this earth as it is in heaven (see Matthew 6:10)?

Whether you have just come to Christ or have been walking with him for a while, decide to be a person with good soil. God has shown us what to do to avoid rocky soil or soil with thorns. His Word teaches us what to do to avoid that kind of soil in our hearts.

In conclusion, we have learned that there are only two destinations for all mankind. They are either eternal punishment or eternal life. Eternal life is a gift from God and is obtained by God's grace through faith. Salvation involves two important aspects, repentance, and faith. We must purpose in our heart to turn away from sin and live a life pleasing to the Lord and this is accomplished through faith in Jesus Christ. Faith is not merely a head knowledge or belief, but a heart knowledge that results in action. We also learned that we need and are saved by God's grace. God's grace cannot be earned but is freely given to those who are humble and have faith.

Everyone who comes to faith in Christ has one of three types of soil in his heart. He either has rocky soil, soil with thorns, or good soil. The one with good soil produces fruit. We must be careful to make sure we have good soil in our heart. We can do this by obeying God's Word concerning trials, worries, pleasures, and wealth.

If you have not already done so, repent of your sins and believe in and receive Jesus Christ into your life as your Lord and Savior. Determine to have "good soil" in your heart. Also, arrange to be baptized as soon as possible. Below is an example of a simple prayer that you can pray to God to be saved. Simply saying a prayer will not save you unless you sincerely mean what you say.

> Dear God, I believe that Jesus Christ is the Son of God. I believe in and receive Jesus into my life. I believe he died to pay the penalty for my sins and then rose from the dead. I confess that I have sinned and am unworthy of heaven. By

your grace, I ask that you forgive me of all my sins because of Christ's sacrifice on the cross to atone for my sin. I turn from my sin and turn to you in repentance and want to live a life that is pleasing to you. I place my faith in Jesus and trust him to save me, forgive my sins, and fill me with the Holy Spirit. Amen.

The scriptural basis for this prayer is as follows:

- Jesus Christ is the Son of God: Mark 1:1
- Believe in and receive Jesus Christ: John 1:12 (and many others)
- Jesus paid the penalty/atoned for our sins: 1 John 2:2
- Jesus rose from the dead: Romans 10:9–10
- I confess that I have sinned: Romans 3:23
- I ask you to forgive me of my sins: 1 John 1:9
- I turn from my sin and turn to you in repentance: Acts 17:30, Matthew 3:8, Acts 3:19; 26:15–20
- And want to live a life that is pleasing to you: Colossians 1:10
- I place my faith in Jesus: Ephesians 2:8
- Fill me with the Holy Spirit: Acts 2:38

If you prayed that prayer and meant it, sign and date it here:

Signature _______________________________
Date _______________________________
Date of baptism _______________________________

SALVATION (PART 2)

When a person comes to faith in Christ and is born again, we refer to that person as having been saved. We speak of salvation in the past tense. It is very important to understand that salvation is not just a thing of the past but is also an ongoing experience. Colossians 2:6–7 states: "So then, just as you received Christ Jesus as Lord, continue to live in him, rooted and built up in him, strengthened in the faith as you were taught, and overflowing with thankfulness" (NIV). So salvation is not a one-time event. It is an ongoing life that is referred to in scripture as a past event, an ongoing present experience, and a future hope. The end result or the outcome of our faith is the salvation of our soul as stated in 1 Peter 1:8–9: "Though you have not seen him, you love him; and even though you do not see him now, you believe in him and are filled with an inexpressible and glorious joy, for you are receiving the goal of your faith, the salvation of your souls" (NIV).

There are three specific terms in the Bible that illustrate the past, present, and future concepts of salvation. They are justification, sanctification, and glorification, and they all have to do with the issue of sin. Justification refers to being declared righteous upon our repentance and trust in Christ for salvation. When we are justified, our past sins are all forgiven. Being declared righteous means that our sins are no longer counted against us. Christ's sacrifice on the cross to pay the penalty for our sin is accessed by our faith in his finished work on the cross.

Sanctification has two aspects—positional and progressive. Upon our initial salvation, we are sanctified as a result of our justification. This is our positional sanctification. Christ took our sins so that he could give us his righteousness. "For our sake, he made him to be sin who knew no sin, so that in him we might become the righteousness of God" (2 Corinthians 5:21).

However, we also begin a process of sanctification which deals with sin in our day-to-day lives and the overcoming of those sins. This is our progressive sanctification. This is where repentance comes in. When we sin, as we all still do, we repent and confess them and ask for God's help in overcoming that sin. Both justification and sanctification are also ongoing characteristics of a believer. When you are working on overcoming the sins in your life (sanctification), you are also confessing those sins and being justified as a result. In 1 John 1:9, it states that when we confess our sins, not only are they forgiven but we are also "purified of all unrighteousness" (justified).

Then there comes glorification when we will be done with sin forever. This happens when we are either raptured or raised from the dead and meet the Lord in the clouds at his return. When the Lord returns to us who are still alive and to those that have already passed away, we will all receive a new imperishable glorified body that cannot sin!

To sum this up, we are set free from the penalty of sin through justification. We are set free from the power of sin in sanctification. And we are altogether set free from sin in our glorification.

Is past, present, or future tense being used in the following passages?

1. Romans 8:24 _______________________________________
2. 1 Corinthians 1:18_________________________________
3. Ephesians 2:8 ____________________________________
4. Matthew 10:21-22 _________________________________
5. 1 Corinthians 15:2 ________________________________
6. 1 Thessalonians 5:9 _______________________________

7.   Romans 13:11 _______________________________________
8.   2 Corinthians 2:15 _________________________________
9.   Matthew 24:13 ______________________________________

One more verse that shows we must continue in faith unto the end is Hebrews 3:14. It says, "For we have come to share in Christ, if indeed we hold our original confidence firm to the end." The obvious implication here is that if we do not hold our confidence to the end, we will not share in Christ. This confirms what Jesus said in Matthew 10:22. It is those who endure to the end that will be saved.

Another concept that demonstrates that our salvation is not complete until our perishable bodies put on the imperishable is the concept of hope. As Romans 8:24 says, "For in this hope we were saved. But hope that is seen is no hope at all. Who hopes for what he already has?" (NIV).

The following verses point out this hope.

In 1 Thessalonians 5:8, Paul writes: "But since we belong to the day, let us be sober, having put on the breastplate of faith and love, and for a helmet the hope of salvation."

And again, "Paul, a servant of God and an apostle of Jesus Christ, for the sake of the faith of God's elect and their knowledge of the truth, which accords with godliness, in hope of eternal life, which God, who never lies, promised before the ages began" (Titus 1:1–2).

Here is another passage that speaks of the hope of eternal life, "But when the goodness and loving kindness of God our Savior appeared, he saved us, not because of works done by us in righteousness, but according to his own mercy, by the washing of regeneration and renewal of the Holy Spirit, whom he poured out on us richly through Jesus Christ our Savior, so that being justified by his grace we might become heirs according to the hope of eternal life" (Titus 3:4–7).

Those three passages point out our hope of salvation. And as Romans 8:24 points out, we do not hope for something we already have.

It is true that at our initial salvation, we are said to have passed from death to life and that we have (present tense) eternal life (John

5:24). Yet scripture speaks of our hope of eternal life and the promise of eternal life. This is a concept called "now but not yet." We currently have eternal life but not yet. We have it because Jesus declared it. Yet we do not yet have it because we are still in our perishable bodies. God, who is outside of time and sees all things, can declare future events as though they have already happened. Romans 8:30 is a good example of this. Here is what it says: "And those whom he predestined he also called, and those whom he called he also justified, and those whom he justified he also glorified."

Glorification is the final stage where we put off our perishable body and put on the imperishable. This is when we are glorified. In Romans 8:30, God speaks of this future event in the past tense. Therefore, it should be no surprise that the Word can declare that we have eternal life, which will be ultimately fulfilled in the future.

In lesson 1, I said that it is critically important that we understand that there are three phases of salvation because it will keep us from doctrinal error that can do much damage to our spiritual well-being. One of those dangers is being lukewarm. If you think your salvation is complete upon justification, you may just "coast" in your Christianity. I suffered many years from a lack of zeal simply because I became comfortable in my salvation. I came to a point where I felt I was doing pretty good. I was not earnestly striving to overcome sin and become more like Christ. When I look back, perhaps I was a bit too lukewarm.

The greatest danger, though, is to believe that once you are initially saved, you can never again be lost. This is dangerous because we won't have to take sin seriously if it doesn't matter in the long run. If we think we will be saved no matter how much sin we become involved in, we are in a dangerous place. It is like we have a "license to sin." This concept of never being able to be lost after initial salvation is often called Once Saved, Always Saved or OSAS. We will examine this concept in more detail in lesson 6.

To sum up salvation, it is something we received upon conversion to Christ (Ephesians 2:8), something we enjoy as we continue to live in Christ (Colossians 2:6), and something we fully realize if we endure to the end (Matthew 10:21–22).

We learned in lesson 1 that the two main ingredients necessary for salvation are repentance and faith in the Lord Jesus Christ. There is a third aspect of salvation that is also very important. It is baptism. If you will recall from lesson 1, Peter declared in Acts 2:38 that everyone should repent and be baptized in the name of Jesus Christ for the forgiveness of sins. However, there has been much debate as to the necessity of baptism for salvation. Let's look at some of the scriptures involved.

10. We have already mentioned Acts 2:38. What is the promise given with baptism? _______________________________

____

11. In Mark 16:16, who is said will be saved? _______________

____

12. In Mark 16:16, who will be condemned? _______________

____

13. What did Jesus instruct his disciples to do in Matthew 28:19? _____________________________________

____

14. What does it say about baptism in 1 Peter 3:19–21? ______

____

____

15. Who or what does Romans 6:4 say we are baptized into?

____

16. In Galatians 3:27, what does Paul say about those who have been baptized into Christ? _______________________

____

17. In Acts 10:44–48, did the Gentiles receive the Holy Spirit before or after they were baptized? _______________

Notice in Romans 6:4 that we are buried with Christ by being baptized into his death. If we are baptized into death, what exactly has died? In Romans 6:6, it states that our old self was crucified with him (Christ). It is through baptism that the body of sin is crucified, or put to death, that it might be done away with or rendered powerless.

In America, it seems we have downplayed the necessity of baptism, and it is sometimes weeks or months after conversion before one is baptized. This should not be. When a person comes to faith in Christ, at the very least they should be told of their need to be baptized as soon as possible. How else would they know that the Bible commands it? Should we wait for them to find it in the Bible for themselves?

What about the case where a person refuses to be baptized? If a person refuses to be baptized, they are refusing to be baptized into Christ (Romans 6:3), refusing to have their sins washed away (Acts 2:38 and 22:16), and may even be refusing the gift of the Holy Spirit (Acts 2:38). By refusing to be baptized, a person is refusing to be united with Christ in his death, burial, and resurrection. Consider what the Old Testament may teach us.

In the Old Testament, circumcision was the sign of the covenant between God and his people. Anyone who was not circumcised was to be cut off from God's people because he had broken God's covenant (see Genesis 17:10–14). In the New Testament, baptism serves as sign of the new covenant between God and his people. Romans 6:3–4 teaches us that when we are baptized, we are baptized into Christ and into his death and that we will also be united to him in resurrection. Also consider Colossians 2:9–12: "For in Christ all the fullness of the Deity lives in bodily form, and you have been given fullness in Christ, who is the head over every power and authority. In him you were also circumcised, in the putting off of the sinful nature, not with a circumcision done by the hands of men but with the circumcision done by Christ, having been buried with him in baptism, and raised with him through your faith in the power of God, who raised him from the dead" (NIV). Notice the connection of circumcision with baptism in this passage. Circumcision in this passage is a figurative one where the sinful nature (or flesh) is being cut off. In the Old Testament, circumcision was literal and done physically in the body to symbolize the covenant between God and his people. In the New Testament, baptism is symbolic of the new covenant with God and equates to a spiritual circumcision in which the sinful nature is cut off. Notice also in the Old Testament a reference to a spiritual circumcision in Jeremiah 4:4: "Circumcise yourselves to the LORD; remove the foreskin of your hearts, O men of Judah and inhabitants of Jerusalem; lest my wrath go forth like fire and burn with none to quench it, because of the evil of your deeds."

Considering how God viewed circumcision under the old covenant and the commands regarding baptism given in the New Testament, would it not be reasonable to conclude that a person that refuses to be baptized should also be "cut off" from God's people just as the uncircumcised were?

So what can we conclude about baptism? Is it required for salvation or not? We see that God requires and commands that a believer be baptized. Several verses tie baptism with salvation. However, many will point out that the thief on the cross, who asked that Jesus remember him, was told by Jesus that he would be in paradise with him that same day. Obviously, the thief was not baptized. Also of note are the Gentiles in Acts 10 that received the Holy Spirit before being baptized. It may also be noteworthy that in Mark 16:16, after stating that those who believe and are baptized will be saved, it only mentions those who do not believe that will be condemned, making no mention of not being baptized.

We could also consider the person who comes to faith in Christ while riding in a car or an airplane. What would happen if that car or airplane crashes, killing all aboard, before that new convert could be baptized? Surely God would not hold him at fault for not being baptized, would he?

In view of these various situations, I believe that a reasoned answer as to whether baptism is required for salvation would be yes and no.

Yes, it is commanded by our Lord and should be done so that we can be united with Christ (Romans 6:5), have our sins washed away (Acts 22:16), receive the Holy Spirit (Acts 2:38), be saved (Mark 16:16, 1 Peter 3:21) and so that the body of sin (in Romans 6:6) might be destroyed (KJV), might be done away with (NKJV, NASB20, and NIV 1984), might lose its power (NLT), might be brought to nothing (ESV), might be rendered powerless (NIV 1978 and CSB) or no longer dominate us (NET).

No, it is not required when a person does not know that he should be baptized, or in cases where a person has not had the opportunity to be baptized before his death, or even when a new convert has not been baptized yet but fully intends to be. It should also be noted that Paul, who preached repentance and faith to both Jew and Gentile, did not baptize anyone besides Crispus, Gaius, and the household of Stephanas. He even stated that Christ did not send him to baptize, but to preach the gospel. See 1 Corinthians 1:14–17.

I would also note that there is no passage of scripture that says, "Be baptized and you will be saved." In the scriptures, baptism is always subsequent to or in conjunction with salvation. Because of this, I find no justification to baptize an infant. We would not baptize an adult who has not been saved through faith in Christ, so why would we baptize an infant that does not even have the ability to come to faith in Christ? We cannot magically turn an unbeliever into a believer by baptizing them.

In summation, if you have not been baptized after coming to faith in Christ, you should arrange to do so as soon as possible!

Before we move on from the topic of baptism, there is one more issue that needs to be addressed. There are those in Christian circles today that contend that baptism is not necessary for salvation because baptism is work, and we know that works do not save us. There seems to be a lot of confusion on the topic of works. Some say that any works of any kind are not necessary for salvation, and indeed, if you believe they are, you are believing in a false gospel because we are not saved by works. Let us look at what the scriptures say about works. In the following passages, depending on what translation you are using, you will find words like acts or deeds instead of works. Those words are all translations of the Greek word *ergon*. *Ergon* is usually translated as works.

18. What kind of works are mentioned in Matthew 5:16?

———————————————————————————

19. What kind of works are mentioned in John 7:7?

———————————————————————————

20. What kind of works are mentioned in John 9:3?

———————————————————————————

21. What kind of works are mentioned in Galatians 2:16?

    ____

22. What kind of works are mentioned in Hebrews 6:1?

    ____

23. What kind of works are mentioned in Galatians 5:19?

    ____

So far, we have listed six different kinds of works. There are more but I just want to include one other. This one is a little more difficult to classify because there is no adjective describing what kind of works are being mentioned. However, it should be evident from the context what kind of works they are.

24. What kind of works is mentioned in James 2:18? _______

    ____

25. Out of the passages above, which is the only kind of works that states that we are not justified by them? _______

    ____

26. In Romans 3:20, what does Paul say about being justified?

    ____

    ____

27. Read Romans 3:21–24, what does Paul say about being justified in verse 24? _______________________________

    ____

28. In Romans 3:28, how are we justified? _______________

    ____

If you ask people whether they think they will go to heaven or not, many will appeal to being a good person. They will undoubtedly be comparing themselves to others who are less "righteous" than they are. Therefore, when compared to others, one may be able to boast about how good they are. By trying to be a good person, they think they will go to heaven. But Jesus declared in Mark 10:18 that there is no one good but God alone. Neither keeping God's laws nor trying to be a good person will get you to heaven. If those things could get you there, you would have something to boast about.

29. By what law does Paul say boasting is excluded in Romans
    3:27? ____

    ____

Some even contend that faith is a "work" which cannot save
you, but Romans 3:27 dispels that notion stating that boasting is
excluded by the law of faith.

Paul is making the case that to be justified, or declared righteous
before God, one must have faith in Christ apart from doing works of
the law. We will never become good enough by our own efforts to be
justified before God, either by obeying God's commands or by trying
to be a good person. This leaves no room for boasting about how
good we are. Paul confirms this in Ephesians 2:8–9, "For by grace
you have been saved through faith. And this is not your own doing;
it is the gift of God, not a result of works, so that no one may boast."

30. What does Paul say about Abraham being justified regard-
    ing works (of the law) in Romans 4:2–3? _______________

    ____

31. In James 2:21, how does James say that Abraham was jus-
    tified? _______________________________________

32. In James 2:22, what was active and made complete by the
    works of Abraham? _______________________________

33. In James 2:23, why was Abraham counted as righteous?

    ____

In Romans 4:3 and James 2:23, both Paul and James quote the
same verse from Genesis 15:6. They both agree that Abraham was
justified because he believed God's promises to him.

To be justified means to be declared righteous. On the one
hand, Abraham was declared righteous apart from works as stated in
Romans 4. On the other hand, Abraham was declared righteous by
his works in James 2. How can this be? There are no contradictions
in the Word of God. Two things that contradict each other cannot
both be true at the same time. So how do we reconcile the appar-

ent contradiction between Paul and James? We have already seen in Romans 3:20 that no one will be justified by works of the law.

34. What does Hebrews 11:17–19 tell us about how Abraham offered his son Isaac on the altar? ________________________

Remember that in 2:21, James asked if Abraham was justified by works when he offered up his son Isaac on the altar. This is a rhetorical question in which the answer is obviously yes!

35. In James, was Abraham justified by works of the law or works of faith? ________________________

There are those that contend that Abraham could not be justified by works because he was justified many years earlier when he believed God's promise to him, and God declared him righteous. This stems from the idea that salvation is complete when a person comes to faith in Christ and is justified. They fail to see that salvation is a lifelong process and it is completely appropriate to say Abraham was justified by works in offering his son on the altar because his faith and works were working together.

36. What is the conclusion that James comes to in James 2:24 after considering the life of Abraham? ________________________
____

37. In James 2:26, what does James say about faith that has no works? ________________________

In James 2:20–24, it speaks of works that are done because of what Abraham believed. James makes no reference to works of the law. He ties together Abraham's faith and works done because of his faith and shows that Abraham's faith was completed by his works. In verse 21, Abraham was justified by his works in offering his son as a sacrifice. As Hebrews 11:17–19, shows, Abraham offered his son on the altar by faith.

Abraham's faith and actions based on faith were working together. Thus, Abraham's faith was made complete by his works.

Abraham's "work" of offering his son on the altar was done in faith because he believed God could or would raise Isaac from the dead if need be. As a result, he was justified, not by works of the law, but by works done in faith.

James goes on to point out that those who have no works (by context of faith) have a dead faith that cannot save. In fact, he plainly states that we are justified by works and not by faith alone. The works he is talking about are works of faith or works that flow from our faith as demonstrated by Abraham. When we look at the context of what Paul was saying about Abraham in Romans, we see that he was making the argument that Abraham was not justified by works of the law. Beginning in Romans 3:21 through 4:9, Paul is contrasting being saved by faith versus works of the law. When we look at James, we see that Abraham was justified by works of faith. Since Paul and James were referring to two distinct kinds of works, there is no contradiction between them.

It is unfortunate that Christians often say that we are saved by faith alone. This is not entirely accurate since James says the exact opposite in 2:24. The sentiment behind being saved by faith alone is that works of the law or efforts at being good cannot save you. Therefore, you are saved by faith apart from any efforts that you could boast about. And this is true! Hence, some say we are saved by faith alone. But, as James points out, if you have no works of faith demonstrating that your faith is genuine, all you have is a dead faith that cannot save. That's why he says we are justified by works and not faith *alone*! Also, remember that the law of faith dictates that your works of faith give you nothing to boast about!

In conclusion, baptism is not a work of the law but a work of faith. Being baptized as a part of salvation is not one of the works that Paul writes to the Ephesians about in chapter 2 or to the Romans in chapter 4 as something we can boast about. We get baptized because of our faith in Christ and want to please him and love him by being obedient to his commands. Jesus told us that if we love him, we will obey his commands. Consequently, baptism is not a work that would discount a person's salvation. It is an act of love for the Lord since it is being done in obedience to the Lord's command to be baptized.

FOUR ESSENTIAL HABITS

In this lesson we will look at four essential habits that you should develop as a disciple of Christ. These are the basics and are very important in learning how to follow Christ and live for him. Christianity is not so much a religion as it is a relationship. Since Christ rose from the dead and is alive forevermore, we can actually interact with him.

1. After Jesus rose from the dead, he ascended into heaven and is no longer physically here on earth. When you repent of your sins and receive him as your Lord and Savior, you establish a relationship with him. Since he can no longer be seen by our human eyes nor heard by our human ears, how do you think you can get to know him and relate to him?

    ____

    ____

    ____

    ____

2. What does 2 Peter 3:18 instruct us to do? _______________

    ____

3. In Titus 2:11–12, what does God's grace teach (or train) us to do? _______________________________________

    ____

Read and Study the Bible

4. In order to grow in the grace and knowledge of Christ, there are four essential habits to help us do so. How did the Word of God come about according to 2 Peter 1:21?

____

5. How did the Word of God come about according to 2 Timothy 3:16?_____________________________

____

6. According to 2 Timothy 3:16, what is the Word of God useful (or profitable) for? ______________________

____

____

7. What does 2 Timothy 2:15 say about the importance of learning what the Bible says? ____________________

____

____

If you are using the KJV or NKJV in looking up 2 Timothy 2:15, you will find that it says we are to rightly divide the word of truth. Dispensationalists like to use this verse to teach that we are to divide up the Word into different dispensations. The Greek word translated *divide* in this passage is *orthotomeo*. This is what W. E. Vines Greek Expository Dictionary has to say about *orthotomeo*: "the meaning passed from the idea of cutting or dividing, to the more general sense of rightly dealing with a thing. What is intended here is not dividing Scripture from Scripture but teaching Scripture accurately."[2] That is how most modern translations interpret it.

If you have a red-letter edition of the Bible, when you read what is typed in red, you will be reading what Christ spoke while he was on earth. Indeed, all scripture is God's message to us. As we read and

---

[2] W. E. Vine, *An Expository Dictionary Of New Testament Words: With Their Precise Meanings For English Readers*, vol. 2, p. 327 (Nashville, Tennessee: T. Nelson Publishers, 1985).

study the Bible, we will be getting to know what God thinks and what he desires for each of us.

When we want to get to know someone, we spend time with them. By doing so, we find out what they like, what their values are, how they think and react to various life situations, and who they really are. When we read and study God's Word, we learn what Jesus likes, what his values are, and who he really is. In John 1:1, Jesus is called the Word of God. Consequently, we can learn of him by reading all the Bible and not just the things recorded of what he said while on earth.

There are other ways to get to know him beside just reading the Bible. For example, we can learn things from the hardships that we go through.

8.   In Hebrews 12:5–6, who is it that disciplines us?

____

9.   In Hebrews 12:7–11, why does God discipline us?

____

____

____

In Hebrews 12:7, the New International Version instructs us to endure hardship as discipline. The Christian Standard Bible and New English Translation tell us to endure suffering as discipline. It is a good practice to pray and ask why you are enduring hardship or suffering. All suffering may not necessarily be discipline from God. Therefore, we should always ask for discernment as to why we are suffering.

When we read and study the Bible, we are actually listening to God. He is telling us everything he wants us to know, especially about ourselves and how we can please him. As we have seen, he has given us commands to be kept and if we do not obey, we may suffer discipline from the Lord as a result.

Listening to someone is very important in getting to know them. God is not limited to the scriptures as a way of speaking to us. There are other ways that we can listen to God and learn from him.

He may be revealing to us his will for us or directing us to go in a different direction. Consider the lives of Jonah and Balaam:

10. What did God tell Jonah to do in Jonah 1:1–2? __________

11. According to Jonah 1:3, what did Jonah do? __________

12. According to Jonah 1:4, what was God's response? __________

In Numbers 22, there is an account of Balak, the king of Moab, who sent messengers to Balaam to ask Balaam to go back with them to curse the Israelites.

13. In Numbers 22:12, what did God tell Balaam to do?

14. Balaam at first did not go with them but eventually, after more messengers from Balak came to him, he did go. How did the Lord respond to Balaam when he went with the messengers from Moab as found in Numbers 22:22–27?

In Jonah's case, the LORD sent a great wind (and a great fish) to oppose Jonah's flight away from Nineveh and in Balaam's case, the LORD opposed Balaam by sending the angel of the LORD to oppose Balaam's donkey (whom Balaam was riding on but could not see the angel of the LORD), and thus oppose Balaam. In both cases, Jonah and Balaam chose to go in a direction other than what the LORD wanted them to. As a result, he put obstacles in their way.

When you find that you are running into obstacles in your path, you might consider that those obstacles may be from the Lord to change your direction. In the case of Jonah and Balaam, it was because of disobedience that God was opposing them and putting obstacles in their way. However, not all obstacles are necessarily due to disobedience. The Lord may just be redirecting you in another direction to show you his will for your life.

Also, not all obstacles are because you are going in the wrong direction. They may just be trials that the Lord is allowing in order to develop patience and/or perseverance in your life. You should always pray for discernment in these situations. This brings us to our next essential habit: prayer.

Prayer

15. Jesus instructed his disciples on how to pray in Matthew 6:9–13. What are the key elements of his prayer? ________

____

____

____

____

16. In Matthew 6:5–8, what other instructions did Jesus give us regarding prayer?____

____

____

17. According to the following passages, who should we pray for?
    a. Matthew 5:44 ______________________________
    b. Luke 6:28 ________________________________
    c. Ephesians 6:18 ___________________________
    d. 1 Timothy 2:1–2 _________________________
    e. Philippians 4:6 __________________________
18. What does God promise to those who pray as found in the following verses?
    a. Mark 11:24 ______________________________
    b. John 14:13–14 ___________________________
    c. John 15:7 ________________________________

God has promised to answer our prayers and grant what we ask for. However, there are also conditions and hindrances to receiving the things we ask for. James tells us two reasons why we do not receive what we ask for in prayer. What are those conditions?

19. In James 4:2–3, what two reasons are given for not receiving what we ask for in prayer?

    a. ____

    b. ____

Just previously, we read Matthew 6:5–8. In verse 8, God says he knows what we need before we even ask him. So then, why do we need to pray about it if God already knows? James tells us that we don't have because we don't ask. Evidently, God wants us to ask him for what we need. He wants to be our provider so that we don't rely on ourselves and thus think that we have provided for ourselves and don't really need him. James 1:17 tells us that every good and perfect gift comes from God above. This is also part of having a relationship with the Lord. We rely on him for all things.

20. 1 John 5:14–15 gives us another condition for answered prayer. What is it? ______________________________
____

21. What is the condition found in Mark 11:24? __________
____

22. What is a hindrance to answered prayer found in Isaiah 59:2 and Psalm 66:18? ___________________________
____

23. What is the hindrance found in 1 Peter 3:7? _________
____

24. In Luke 18:1–5, what does Jesus teach his disciples about how to pray? ___________________________________
____
____

In Romans 4:18–21 we have an amazing story about Abraham. Abraham believed God's promise to him that Sarah would bear a son. That promise took many years to come to fruition, but the amazing thing is that not only did Abraham continue to believe the promise, but he did not weaken in his faith. In fact, in verse 20 we are told that he did not waver concerning the promise but rather, his faith grew stronger. I think the lesson we can learn from Abraham is that when we pray in faith for something we believe to be God's will, we should persevere in that faith. I will only add one disclaimer: it may be that God will not answer due to something else. Perhaps you have unforgiveness in your heart toward a brother or a husband is not treating his wife with respect, etc. Therefore, it is important that we consider all the hindrances to prayer and correct them as we persevere in prayer. God's answer may still be no for reasons beyond our knowledge. In that situation, you might also pray for discernment as to how long you persevere in prayer.

25. In view of the scriptures we have studied, how would you sum up what an effective prayer life would look like?

____

____

____

____

____

The title to the Book of Acts is often used as an acronym on how to pattern your prayers. The letter A stands for adoration. The letter C stands for confession. The letter T stands for thanksgiving, and the letter S stands for supplication (to make a humble plea or petition).

It is a good habit to begin your day in prayer before you start your daily activities. I would also suggest that it is a good idea to also pray before retiring for the evening. If you use ACTS as a guideline for your prayers, in the morning, you could spend some time in adoration of God and praising him for who he is. Also, you could present your requests to God (supplication). This is the A and the S of ACTS.

In the evening, you could reflect back upon your day and confess any sins you become aware of and then also give thanks in everything. This would be a great time to think upon your morning prayer requests and give thanks for any answers you received during the day. This is the C and the T of ACTS.

Of course, it is best to confess our sins as soon as we can, but sometimes we are not aware of our sin until we reflect back upon our day. The same goes for thanksgiving. It is better to be thankful all day long rather than just in the evening. Work to develop an attitude of thanksgiving in all you do.

Fellowship

26. What four things did the disciples do as recorded in Acts 2:42?

    a. _______________________________________

    b. _______________________________________

    c. _______________________________________

    d. _______________________________________

27. Hebrews 10:25 instructs us to do two things. What are those?

    a. _______________________________________

    b. _______________________________________

28. In 1 John 1:3, who else is our fellowship with? _________
    ____

Fellowship is very important to a person's spiritual growth. Make time to join with other believers in fellowship. By doing so, you learn more about God and his Word. You also become accountable to each other and help each other grow in the faith. Our most important fellowship is with the Father and his Son Jesus Christ.

Sharing Your Faith

Once a person is born again and has been saved, it is natural for them to want their friends and loved ones to also be saved. The effort to bring them into a saving knowledge of Jesus Christ is what we call evangelism. To evangelize means to preach the gospel to or to convert to Christianity. God has called some to the ministry of evangelism (Ephesians 4:11–13), but we can all evangelize even though we have not been specifically called to that ministry.

29. The essence of the gospel is summed up in 1 Corinthians 15:1–4. According to this passage, what are the three essential elements of the gospel message? _______________________

____

Recall from our first lesson that repentance is also an important step in salvation. Also, recall from our second lesson the importance of baptism. Even though baptism may technically not be required to initially be saved, it is an important first step in beginning the Christian life.

30. What did the Apostle Paul declare to both Jews and Gentiles in Acts 20:21? _______________________

____

31. In Acts 26:19–20, what did Paul specifically say should be done in regard to repentance? _______________________

____

32. How could you use John 3:3 and 5 coupled with John 1:12–13 to share the gospel? _______________________

____

____

____

The four essential habits for a Christian are reading the Word, prayer, fellowship with other believers, and sharing your faith with unbelievers. The first two are usually incorporated into a time of daily devotions. It is important to spend some time each day in reading the Word and prayer. When you read the Word, God is speaking to you, and when you pray, you are speaking to God. If you want to read through the entire Bible, reading only three to four chapters a day will get you all the way through in a year.

It is helpful to establish a set time and place for a daily devotional which will help you get into a habit of spending quality time with the Lord. It should be a time when distractions will be at a minimum and you are not overly tired. Choosing a specific place helps you to form the habit of having a devotional time along with putting you in the proper frame of mind. Setting a time in the morning before you start your day is always a good option. Whatever time and place you choose is up to you. But do not feel guilty if you must miss devotions on a particular day. It should be a time of joy in fellowshipping with the Lord and not a legalistic endeavor.

If you have not already chosen a time and place for devotions, commit to one now.

Time: _______________________________

Place: _______________________________

SANCTIFICATION

As a result of Adam's fall into sin, we have all inherited a sinful nature (often referred to as our flesh). As a result, we all sin which ends in physical death as pointed out in Romans 5:12, "Therefore, just as sin came into the world through one man, and death through sin, and so death spread to all men because all sinned." Not only do we sin, but we are slaves to sin as Romans 6:20 declares: "For when you were slaves of sin, you were free in regard to righteousness."

When a person comes to faith in Christ, he dies to sin and should no longer live in it. Romans 6:1–2 teaches us what our attitude should be toward sin now that we are born again: "What shall we say then? Are we to continue in sin that grace may abound? By no means! How can we who died to sin still live in it?" And the good news is that we are no longer a slave to sin: "For sin will have no dominion over you, since you are not under law but under grace" (Romans 6:14). Consider what we are told about sin in Romans 6:6–7: "For we know that our old self was crucified with him so that the body of sin might be done away with, that we should no longer be slaves to sin—because anyone who has died has been freed from sin."

This lesson will give us some key insights into how to deal with sin in our lives.

God's Purpose for Your Life

Once you are born again, you are a child of God. You now have a relationship with him through his Son.

1. As your heavenly father, what is God's purpose for you as found in Romans 8:28–29? _______________________

    ____

2. What is God's purpose for you as found in 1 Thessalonians 5:23? _______________________________________

    ____

Sanctification has two aspects. One is positional sanctification, and the other is progressive sanctification. When we place our trust in Christ to save us, we are positionally sanctified. We are holy in God's sight because of what Christ has done for us by his sacrifice on the cross, bearing our sins so that we can be forgiven. Because of this, Christ imputes to us his righteousness. But in our day-to-day walk, we still sin. This is where progressive sanctification comes in. We are to deal with and overcome the sin in our lives. In the following passages, tell which speak of our positional sanctification and which speak of our progressive sanctification.

3. Hebrews 10:8–10 _______________________________
4. Philippians 2:12–13 ____________________________
5. 2 Corinthians 5:21 _____________________________
6. 1 Corinthians 1:2 ______________________________
7. 1 Corinthians 6:11 _____________________________
8. Colossians 3:5–8 _______________________________
9. 1 Peter 1:2 ____________________________________

The first part in the process of progressive sanctification is to confess our sins. There are some in Christian circles today that are teaching that when we come to Christ, our sins are all forgiven, including our future sins. They even teach that God does not even see the sins we commit since he sees us as holy and completely sanctified in Christ. They argue that since Christ died over two thousand years ago, all our sins were future at that point. That is true. But then they go on to assert that when we become a Christian, all our future sins are also already forgiven. Therefore, there is no need to even confess our current sins since they have already been forgiven. This comes from a misunderstanding of the two sides of sanctification. They acknowledge positional sanctification, but not progressive.

It is a mistaken idea that Christ died for the forgiveness of our sins. He died to atone for our sins, and it is only when we confess our sins and ask to be forgiven that the forgiveness of our sins is applied. So, though it is true that when Christ died on the cross two thousand years ago, all our sins were still future. It is also true that as far as we are concerned, when we come to faith in Christ, all our sins to that point are in the past. Upon our repentance and faith in Christ, all those past sins are forgiven through the shed blood of Christ. Listen to 1 John 2:2, "He is the atoning sacrifice for our sins, and not only for ours but also for the sins of the whole world." He died to atone for sin so that the whole world could be forgiven of them. If he died for the forgiveness of our sins and he died "for the sins of the whole world," then there would be universal salvation. But there is not universal salvation. Therefore, forgiveness is available to the whole world because of the atonement, but only those who avail themselves of it through faith in Christ will be forgiven.

To see all our future sins as already forgiven is a serious error. What would be the point of acknowledging our sins, confessing them, or even being concerned about them if God has already forgiven them and sees us as holy? He does see us as holy, but that is our positional sanctification. Christ became sin for us so that we could become righteous in God's sight. "For our sake he made him to be sin who knew no sin, so that in him we might become the righteousness of God" (2 Corinthians 5:21). Christ took our sins and gave us his righteousness. That is our position in Christ. In our daily lives, however, we certainly must admit that we still do sin. When we do, we must take heed of 1 John 1:9, which says, "If we confess our sins, he is faithful and just to forgive us our sins and to cleanse us from all unrighteousness."

All throughout the Old and New Testaments, it is clear that God desires his people to be holy and obedient to his commands. He does not save us so that we can then go on in our sin without concern or consequence.

We must be willing to acknowledge to God that we have fallen short of his standard of holiness and are willing to change. There is a big difference between Jesus's atoning for our sins and forgiving our sins. When we repent of our past sins (which were all future when Christ died for them) and place our faith in Christ, all our past sins to that point are then forgiven because of the atonement.

From that point on, we must deal with our present sins and overcome them that we might be holy as he is holy. There is no need to forgive us of sins we have not committed. To say they are forgiven before we even commit them is coming dangerously close to giving a license to sin. What would your school-age child think if you told him that you have already forgiven him for cheating on his math test that he will take tomorrow? Wouldn't he get the impression that it is ok with you that he goes ahead and cheats?

This kind of teaching is contrary to the idea that we need to be involved in progressive sanctification and stunts our growth in Christlikeness.

10. What are we promised in 1 John 1:9? ______________________

There is no need to give us this promise if our sins have already been forgiven. In fact, if all our future sins were forgiven upon conversion, the verse would read something like this: "There is no need to confess our sins, because they have already been forgiven." Instead, it says, "If we confess." The verse is a conditional statement. There is a condition, confessing our sins, and a consequence—being forgiven. We have already seen in our prayer lives that if we harbor sin in our life, God will not hear our prayers. Sin causes a break in our fellowship with God. In lesson 6, we will discuss the serious end result if we continue to sin deliberately.

We resolve a break in our fellowship with God by confessing our sins. When we do so, we are restored to fellowship with the Lord.

Isn't this also true in our human relationships? When we offend someone, doesn't that hinder our relationship with them until the offense has been dealt with?

The first thing we must understand about sin and temptation is whether temptation itself is a sin.

11. Does Hebrews 4:15 teach that temptation is a sin? _______
12. What does God promise us in 1 Corinthians 10:13 concerning temptation? _______________________________
____

We can see from questions 11 and 12 that temptation is not sin. Christ was sinless yet was tempted as we are. He said no to temptation.

You will probably find in your Christian experience (we call it our walk) that Satan will work through your desires to tempt you to fall into sin. He also works on your mind since he is a liar and tries to deceive you whenever he can. However, many of our fleshly desires cause us to sin and that is what Satan uses to tempt us to sin.

God will usually work through our minds. Read James 1:13–15 and answer the following questions.

13. How is a person tempted? _______________________
14. What does your desire lead to? _________________
15. What does sin lead to? _________________________
16. What does Romans 12:2 say about our mind?
____
____
____

17. In 2 Corinthians 10:5, what does Paul say that we do?
____
____

When our evil desires are causing us to think about how we can fulfill those desires, we must take those thoughts captive. What does that mean and how do we do that? It is really very simple. Once you recognize that you have impure thoughts, you simply stop those thoughts by thinking about something else. You could think about your plans for the weekend or what you are going to have for dinner or a host of other life activities. One of the most effective ways to change your thinking is to resort to prayer. For example, if you are being tempted by lust, you can start praying for the person you are being tempted by. Pray for their salvation. Pray that God would bless them. And of course, avert your eyes. You might just find that when you begin praying for them, Satan may leave you alone! Resist the devil and he will flee from you (James 4:7).

It should be noted that though Satan will work through our sinful desires to tempt us to sin, he also works on our minds. Satan is a liar and a deceiver. He seeks to lead you astray from God through lies and deception. He works through desires to tempt us to sin, and he works through lies and deception to lead us away from God.

God's Power for Your Life

We have seen that God will not allow us to be tempted beyond what we can bear but will provide a way out for us when we are tempted.

18. What two resources have we been given to enable us to live a life that is pleasing to God as found in 2 Peter 1:3–4?

    ____

    ____

19. In Acts 2:38, what is another resource that we have been given? _______________________________________

20. What tool do we have available according to James 5:16?

    ____

21. In Romans 6:3–7, what has Jesus done for us? __________

    ____

Hebrews 8:6–10 tells us that the new covenant is better than the old covenant because it is founded on better promises. According to 2 Peter 1:4, those better promises enable us to partake of God's divine nature. Acts 2:38 promises us the Holy Spirit, which manifests the divine power mentioned in 2 Peter 1:3. He enables us to escape the corruption of this world. Jesus broke the power of sin in our lives by dying and rising again from the dead. He conquered sin and death for us that we might do the same. Finally, it is through prayer that we can access that divine power and those precious promises to help us in our process of sanctification!

God's Plan for Your Life

We have seen that God's ultimate desire for your life is to become like his Son. Also, he has given us all the necessary tools to be able to accomplish that goal. Before we look at how we can specifically work toward that goal, we need to address some issues that may hinder our efforts. We have already mentioned that the first step in this process is to confess our sins.

22. In Psalm 66:18, why is it necessary to confess our sins.

____

____

23. In Mark 11:25, why is forgiving others important?

____

____

24. In 1 Peter 5:5, what sin would greatly hinder our sanctification and why? ____________________________

____

25. In 1 John 2:15, what sin hinders our sanctification?

____

____

26. According to James 4:4, why is the sin of 1 John 2:15 so serious? ________________________________

____

After looking at hindrances that would impede our growth in grace, how do we bring about the changes that God would desire in our lives? What is our part in this process and what is God's?

27. According to Philippians 2:12–13, who is responsible for making changes in our life? _______________________________

____

____

I find the principle found in these two verses to be very important. There is to be a cooperation between us and God. We are commanded to work out our salvation, and when we do, God will work in us to enable us to live a life pleasing to him. It seems many false teachings have arisen in Christianity that do not recognize this principle. Either they put too much emphasis on man's responsibility or on God's responsibility.

Some put man down to the point that we are totally incapable of anything good. Therefore, God is doing all the work. There is a good case to be made for man's depravity, but some even apply this to believers. This always sounds so holy and righteous because by putting ourselves down, we are exalting God in the process. Truly, God should be exalted, but to say a believer is incapable of pleasing God because of our utter sinfulness is nothing but false humility. How could it be that believers who are indwelt by the Holy Spirit would be totally incapable of anything good? Does the Spirit have no power? Remember, Christ broke the power of sin in our lives so that we no longer need to live in them.

We have already seen in questions 18–21 that God has given us the tools to live a life worthy of him. Consider what Colossians 1:9–10 says about our ability to live a life worthy of the Lord and please him in every way. "For this reason, since the day we heard about you, we have not stopped praying for you asking God to fill you with the knowledge of his will through all spiritual wisdom and understanding. And we pray this in order that you may live a life worthy of the Lord and please him in every way: bearing fruit in every good work, growing in the knowledge of God" (NIV).

The other end of the spectrum is placing too much emphasis on man's effort. Paul wrote to the Galatians and called them foolish for trying to be perfected by the flesh after receiving the Spirit. Galatians 3:1–3: "You foolish Galatians! Who has bewitched you? Before your very eyes Jesus Christ was clearly portrayed as crucified. I would like to learn just one thing from you: Did you receive the Spirit by observing the law, or by believing what you heard? Are you so foolish? After beginning with the Spirit, are you now trying to attain your goal by human effort?" (NIV). It is truly foolish to attempt to be holy in our own strength.

We must always remember that when we are working out our salvation, we are to do it in reliance upon the Holy Spirit and his help as promised in Philippians 2:13.

28. Ephesians 4:20–24 describes the sanctification process. Explain how it works. _______________________

____

____

____

____

What are we to put off and put on according to the following verses?

29. Ephesians 4:25
   Off: ____
   On: ____
30. Ephesians 4:28
   Off: ____
   On: ____
31. Ephesians 4:29
   Off: ____
   On: ____
32. Ephesians 4:31–32
   Off: ____
   On: ____

33. Romans 13:12
    Off: ____
    On: ____
34. Colossians 3:8–9 and 12–14
    Off: ____
    On: ____

How exactly do we effect the changes in our life? Remember the power God has given us. He has given us great power in prayer and the Holy Spirit. Use them! As you work out your salvation (Philippians 2:12), God will work in you through your faith in him (Philippians 2:13). Never try to bring about the change in your life through your own efforts.

In summary, to gain victory over sin, you should do the following:

1. Be born again through repentance of sin and faith in Jesus Christ.
2. Ask for the forgiveness of your sins and be baptized.
3. Forgive others that have offended you in any way.
4. Pray in faith, asking for God's help in overcoming sin.
5. Put off the old nature and replace it by putting on the new nature.
6. Persevere in your efforts to overcome sin.
7. Do what pleases the Lord!

Examine yourself and see if there is anyone that you have not forgiven. Forgive them from your heart and tell God that you forgive them. Do this every time thoughts of unforgiveness creep back in.

Make sure you have confessed your sins, making special note to confess any pride or love of this world. Of course, you can ask God to forgive you of ALL your sins and he will. However, when you begin the process of sanctification, you must deal with specific sins.

Choose a specific sin and begin the process of put off and put on. Pray in faith asking God to help you overcome that sin by the power of the Holy Spirit in you. You may find that when you focus on a specific sin, you will have more trouble with it and be tempted more often by it. This may be simply because you are focusing more on it. Do not be discouraged by this. If you are to overcome a sin, you must face it and deal with it. God is working with you to help you.

If a thief is thrown in jail, he is still a thief even though he no longer has an opportunity to steal anything. He will return to his old ways once he is out of jail and has opportunity to steal again. It is only when the thief is changed on the inside that he no longer steals. It is when he is tempted to steal and has the opportunity to steal but refrains and says no to the temptation and puts on the godly alternative that he has truly changed. We must face temptation so that we can learn to resist it and overcome it. It is also at the time of temptation that we can learn to "put on" the biblical alternative!

The principles to overcome sin that are given in this lesson are general principles that will work with any sin. There are innumerable ways of dealing with sin in the process of putting them off. For example, if someone wants to break the addiction to alcohol, they might make sure they do not walk past a bar where they might smell the alcohol and be tempted. They also might make sure that when they go out to eat, they do not go to restaurants that sell alcohol. They might also find an accountability partner that they can call when they are tempted. Perhaps one of the best ways is to stop associating with those who drink.

These ideas are just a few suggestions on how to overcome alcoholism. If you are having great difficulty in dealing with a sin, perhaps you should seek out a Christian counselor. The Christian counselor could act as an accountability partner as well as give you solid biblical advice on overcoming your problems!

You should avoid secular counselors as they do not comprehend the sin nature and how to deal with it. In fact, they might give you ungodly advice that compounds the problem. Most secular counselors believe that man is basically good. How can they deal with sin when they think we are basically good and that society is to blame for our problems?

Persevere!

LESSON 5

YOUR RELATIONSHIP WITH GOD

The world teaches that many of man's problems stem from a lack of self-esteem. Since the 1940s, secular psychology has pushed this idea upon us. Terms such as *self-love, self-regard, positive self-image,* and *self-worth* are all synonymous with self-esteem. This concept was virtually unheard of in Evangelical circles until the mid-1970s. But since that time there has been a flood of Christian teachers and churches that are teaching the importance of self-esteem or self-love. They will use Matthew 22:39 as their primary reason for saying we should love ourselves.

1. Who does Matthew 22:39 teach that we should love?

    ____

2. And how should we love them? ______________________

3. What does Ephesians 5:29 say about loving ourselves?

    ____

    ____

The preceding two verses demonstrate that we already do love ourselves. We feed ourselves, clothe ourselves, find shelter and engage in activities that bring pleasure to ourselves, even when some of those activities may be harmful. Nowhere in scripture are we instructed to love ourselves. Instead, our focus should be on others.

4. What should our attitude be toward others as found in Philippians 2:3? _______________________________

    ____

5. How does the bible describe those who love themselves as found in 2ⁿᵈ Timothy 3:1-5? _______________________________

    ____

    ____

    ____

    ____

We are instructed to avoid people who are lovers of self, lovers of money, and lovers of pleasure rather than of God.

Dictionary.com defines self-esteem as "an inordinately or exaggeratedly favorable impression of oneself."[3]

Pride is defined as "a high or inordinate opinion of one's own dignity, importance, merit, or superiority, whether as cherished in the mind or as displayed in bearing, conduct, etc.; the state or feeling of being proud; a becoming or dignified sense of what is due to oneself or one's position or character; self-respect; self-esteem."[4]

Synonyms of self-esteem would be pride, pridefulness, egotism, conceit and self-regard among others.

We can see from these definitions that pride and self-esteem are synonymous to each other.

6. In Luke 18:10–14, Jesus tells a parable about two men that were praying. Answer the following questions about the two men:

    a. Who were they? _______________________________
    b. Which one went home justified? _______________________________
    c. What happens to the one that exalts himself?

    ____

---

[3] "Self-Esteem Definition & Meaning," Dictionary.com, https://www.dictionary.com/browse/self-esteem#synonym-study.

[4] "Pride Definition & Meaning," Dictionary.com, https://www.dictionary.com/browse/pride.

d.   What happens to the one who humbles himself?

____

Which of the two men in Luke 18 do you think had good self-esteem and which one had poor self-esteem? Please note how God dealt with each man.

7.   In James 4:6, what does God do to the proud?

____

8.   In James 4:6, what does God give to the humble?

____

Man's problem is not that his self-esteem is too low. Rather, it is probably too high. God opposes those who have high self-esteem and humbles them. It is much better to humble yourself and to be given God's grace and be exalted by God rather than to try to exalt yourself!

A Biblical View of Self

9.   In the following verses, how does the Bible describe people before they come to Christ?
    a.   Romans 3:10_______________________________________
    b.   Romans 3:12_______________________________________
    c.   Romans 3:23_______________________________________
    d.   Romans 7:14_______________________________________
    e.   Romans 8:7 _______________________________________
    f.   Romans 8:8 _______________________________________
10.   What does the bible say about those who are in Christ?
    a.   1 John 3:2-3 _______________________________________
    b.   2 Corinthians 5:17 _______________________________________
    c.   2 Corinthians 5:21 _______________________________________
    d.   Galatians 4:7_______________________________________
    e.   Romans 8:15 _______________________________________
    f.   Romans 6:6–7 _______________________________________

Discovering God's Will for Your Life

11. What three things are God's will for you as found in 1 Thessalonians 5:16–18?

    a. ______________________________________

    b. ______________________________________

    c. ______________________________________

12. What is God's will for you in 1 Thessalonians 4:3–7? (See also 1 Peter 1:15–16.)

    ____

    ____

    ____

13. What is God's will for you as found in Romans 8:29?

    ____

    ____

14. What does Romans 12:1–2 tell us about discerning God's will? ______________________________________

    ____

    ____

We have looked at some general characteristics that God wants us to exhibit. But how do we find God's will for specific situations in our lives? There are innumerable things in which we would like God to tell us what to do. Who do we marry? What kind of job should we have? Where should we live? Which house should we buy? Which church should we attend? The list is endless.

Of course, the first thing you should do is pray and ask God for wisdom. James 1:5–6 says: "If any of you lacks wisdom, he should ask God, who gives generously to all without finding fault, and it will be given to him. But when he asks, you must believe and not doubt, because he who doubts is like a wave of the sea, blown and tossed by the wind" (NIV). Believe this promise from God as you work through your decision-making process.

Recall from lesson 3 that God will sometimes put obstacles in our way when we are going in the wrong direction. The examples given were of Jonah and Balaam. If you find many obstacles when you are heading toward a certain decision, this might be a message from the Lord that you are making a mistake.

Another tool in finding God's will in specific situations is to consider Proverbs 15:22. It says, "Plans fail for lack of counsel, but with many advisers they succeed" (NIV). Talk to others of whom you trust and ask for their advice. In prayer, weigh what each had to say, remembering that God has promised you wisdom.

God may even speak through an unbeliever. Remember that he even used a donkey to speak to Balaam! I remember a time in my life when someone said something to me, and I immediately knew that it was from the Lord. I had not asked for advice or even mentioned what I had been praying about. It was said in the normal course of conversation, but I knew it was from the Lord!

One of the best ways that I have found to discern God's will on a given issue is to do what I learned from a cassette tape put out by Pat Robertson many years ago. He suggested that when you are praying about something, you should "have no mind in the matter." In other words, be willing to accept God's answer whatever it may be. Often, our ability to discern God's will is clouded by our own desires. If we truly reach a point where we are willing to accept whatever answer God gives us, we are freed to know his will.

How to Overcome Anxiety in Your Life

In the following passages, consider how God instructs us to handle anxiety?

15. In Philippians 4:4–7, what are the four things you are instructed to do?

    a. ____

    b. ____

    c. ____

    d. ____

16. If you do those four things, what are you promised? ______
____

17. What are we told to do in 1 Peter 5:6–7? ______________

____

Many believers do pray and cast their cares upon the Lord, but then shortly take those cares back upon themselves and begin being anxious or worried all over again. In any situation that you may be anxious or worried about, there are usually things that you can do to relieve those concerns and then there are things that only God can do. For example, let's say you have a third-grade child in school that is not doing well academically. You are anxious about that and ask God to help him to succeed in school. Your part could be to help him with his homework, make sure he gets the necessary sleep, a good breakfast, and is properly dressed for the environment. You are to get him to school on time and prepared to do well. From there on, you must trust God to work out the circumstances. Perhaps the Lord will help your child to pay attention or have the teacher move a disruptive child away from yours. These are things beyond your control. Therefore, do all the things you can to help your child be successful and let God do the things that you can't. Trust him because he says that he cares for you! It does you no good to worry about things that only God can do. Therefore, leave that part to him.

Jesus tells us in John 10:10 that he came to give us a full rich abundant life. When we follow the instructions in God's Word, we experience that abundant life. We will live a life free of anxiety and full of joy, peace, and love!

ONCE SAVED, ALWAYS SAVED?

Christians have debated for centuries whether a person who has genuinely been saved could ever lose that salvation and suffer the same fate as all unbelievers. Let us clarify the issues and try to make some sense of it all. Entire books have been written on this subject, so this will be a very brief exploration of the topic. Before we begin, let it be clear that all scripture is truth. It is "God breathed." There are verses that support both sides of this issue, but one thing we cannot do is deny the truth of either set of verses. After careful examination of both sides, we will try to harmonize the scriptures without denying the truth of any of them. Let us explore this issue with an open mind. And remember, "If anyone imagines that he knows something, he does not yet know as he ought to know" (1 Corinthians 8:2). And "Above all, keep loving one another earnestly, since love covers a multitude of sins" (1 Peter 4:8).

Before we begin, let's make something clear. Salvation is not something you can lose, which could imply that someone or something else could take it from you. We know from John 10 that no one can snatch us out of God's hand. I find no scripture to the contrary. Unfortunately, many people, after reading that no one can snatch us out of God's hand, add "not even you." That doesn't even make sense linguistically and is not in the verse, which makes it a classic case of eisegesis.

Rather than ask if a person can lose their salvation, it would be scripturally more accurate to ask if a person can forfeit their salvation. We know from the first two lessons that we gain eternal life when we choose to repent of our sins and trust Christ for salvation. When we hear the gospel through the Word of Christ and we believe, the result is being justified and born again.

We have also discovered that being justified is just the beginning of salvation. Our salvation will not be complete or fully realized until we put off our perishable body and receive a new imperishable one. The fact that salvation is a lifelong process should indicate that there may be a possibility of something happening along the way that might derail the outcome. If that possibility exists, we should want to understand how it could happen and avoid it at all costs.

Let's begin our study by seeing what Paul teaches on the subject. Consider what Paul writes in 1 Corinthians 9:22–27, "To the weak I became weak, that I might win the weak. I have become all things to all people, that by all means I might save some. I do it all for the sake of the gospel, that I may share with them in its blessings. Do you not know that in a race all the runners run, but only one receives the prize? So run that you may obtain it. Every athlete exercises self-control in all things. They do it to receive a perishable wreath, but we an imperishable. So I do not run aimlessly; I do not box as one beating the air. But I discipline my body and keep it under control, lest after preaching to others I myself should be disqualified."

1. In verse 24, how does Paul characterize the Christian life?

    ____

2. In verse 27, what is Paul concerned about? _______________

In Paul's letter to the Philippians in chapter 3, Paul talks about his righteousness under the law versus his righteousness by faith in Christ. Here is what he says in verses 3–14. "For it is we who are the circumcision, we who worship by the Spirit of God, who glory in Christ Jesus, and who put no confidence in the flesh—though

I myself have reasons for such confidence. If anyone else thinks he has reasons to put confidence in the flesh, I have more: circumcised on the eighth day, of the people of Israel, of the tribe of Benjamin, a Hebrew of Hebrews; in regard to the law, a Pharisee; as for zeal, persecuting the church; as for legalistic righteousness, faultless. But whatever was to my profit I now consider loss for the sake of Christ. What is more, I consider everything a loss compared to the surpassing greatness of knowing Christ Jesus my Lord, for whose sake I have lost all things. I consider them rubbish, that I may gain Christ and be found in him, not having a righteousness of my own that comes from the law, but that which is through faith in Christ—the righteousness that comes from God and is by faith. I want to know Christ and the power of his resurrection and the fellowship of sharing in his sufferings, becoming like him in his death, and so, somehow, to attain to the resurrection from the dead. Not that I have already obtained all this, or have already been made perfect, but I press on to take hold of that for which Christ Jesus took hold of me. Brothers, I do not consider myself yet to have taken hold of it. But one thing I do: Forgetting what is behind and straining toward what is ahead, I press on toward the goal to win the prize for which God has called me heavenward in Christ Jesus" (NIV).

3. In verses 10 and 11, what 5 things does Paul want? _______

____

____

____

____

4. In verses 12 and 13, does Paul think that he has already obtained those 5 things? _______________________________

Please note that the last thing Paul wanted in verse 11 was to attain to the resurrection of the dead. He does not consider to have attained that yet since he is still in his perishable body.

5. What was Paul's desire expressed in Acts 20:24? _________

____

6.   In 2 Timothy 4:7, what did Paul say he had done? _________

____

Paul drew a comparison of the Christian life to a race. In 1 Corinthians 9:24, he spoke about running the race to win. In Philippians 3, he did not consider that he had already finished the race but was pressing on toward the goal. In Acts 20:24, Paul's desire was to finish the race (NIV) and in 2 Timothy 4:7, he declared that he had finished the race and kept the faith. In 1 Corinthians 9:27, Paul was concerned that after preaching to others, he himself might be disqualified. When running a race, if you are disqualified, you do not finish the race. You win no prize.

The Greek word for disqualified is *adokimos*. *Adokimos* is defined as disqualified, rejected, reprobate, one failing the test, or castaway. Paul writes in 2 Corinthians 13:5: "Examine yourselves as to whether you are in the faith. Test yourselves. Do you not know yourselves, that Jesus Christ is in you? Unless indeed you are disqualified" (NKJV). The word disqualified in this verse is again the same Greek word *adokimos*.

7.   Why does Paul tell us to examine ourselves? ____________

____

8.   What do we know if we are not disqualified? ___________

____

9.   What do we know if we are disqualified? ______________

____

In 1 Corinthians, Paul was concerned that after preaching to others, he himself might be disqualified—*adokimos*. In 2 Corinthians, Paul writes that to be disqualified—*adokimos*—means that Christ is not in you and you are not in the faith. Paul clearly recognized that initial salvation, being justified, does not guarantee that you will persevere to the end. And I would note, no one can claim that Paul was never really saved to begin with!

Paul recognizes that the Christian life is one that should be lived in such a way as to win a race. A person should discipline himself in order to win. Paul realized that the race is a lifelong pursuit. One must not be disqualified or he would be rejected or reprobate. Paul believed a person could fall away and not finish the race. We will look at several other passages where Paul makes this idea clear.

There are two trains of thought regarding the idea that once you are saved, you will never lose out on eternal life. The first is that once you are saved, you will always be saved or OSAS. The idea behind this is that when you are born again, you receive the (free) gift of eternal life. You have passed from death to life, and nothing can ever change that. You are guaranteed eternal life no matter what you do or what happens from then on. This is basically teaching that initial salvation is also the completion of salvation as far as eternal life is concerned—no race to run, no perseverance, no keeping the faith necessary or absolutely required in order to receive eternal life.

The other teaching on never losing salvation comes from John Calvin and is called the perseverance of the saints. His theology teaches that God will keep you and since he also teaches that you cannot resist God, you will never lose out on eternal life because God guarantees that he will keep you. There is nothing you could do to alter the outcome.

David Pawson in his book *Once Saved, Always Saved?* writes this concerning what he has coined the "alpha" view:

> This is the simple understanding of OSAS. Its proponents believe that once faith in Christ has been exercised, a person is safe and secure for eternity, no matter what happens afterwards. To put it another way, one moment of faith in a whole lifetime, is sufficient to secure a place in glory. Only the first step is absolutely necessary. You only need to begin at the beginning.
>
> All one needs to do is start the Christian life. You are now "saved." You have a guaranteed ticket to

heaven. Everything is settled. To start is in a sense
to finish.[5]

Let's start by examining the OSAS teaching. What are the impli-
cations of the idea that once you are saved, you can never under any
circumstances miss out on eternal life? Doesn't this mean that you
could sin as much as you want and there would only be disciplinary
consequences from the Lord but not loss of eternal life? Hebrews
3:12 says, "Take care, brothers, lest there be in any of you an evil,
unbelieving heart, leading you to fall away from the living God."
According to OSAS, if you don't take care and do develop an evil
unbelieving heart that falls away from the living God, you will still
enjoy eternal life with this God you have fallen away from.

Another scenario would be that you could go back to trying
to be justified by works of the law and still be saved. This is what
Paul warned the Galatians about. There were Judaizers among the
churches of Galatia that were teaching that it is okay to have faith in
Jesus, but you must also keep the law to be saved. Paul states that if
you go back to the observance of the law for salvation, Christ will be
of no value to you. You will be severed from Christ, and you will fall
from grace.

Let's consider one more implication of OSAS. Christians who
will be alive at the time of the antichrist will be required to take the
mark of the beast and worship him. If they don't, they will not be
able to buy or sell anything without that mark. According to OSAS,
if you take that mark, you will still have eternal life with Christ. Yet
Revelation 14 is very clear that if you take the mark, you will be tor-
mented with fire and sulfur forever and ever in the presence of the
angels and the Lamb.

If we take OSAS to its extreme, wouldn't the logical conclusion
be that you can become a totally reprobate person and still have eternal life. Some years back, I had an email conversation with a person
named Eric Neuman who claimed to be a dispensationalist. I asked

---

[5]   David Pawson, *Once Saved, Always Saved?*, p. 9 (Great Britain: Hodder and
Stoughton Ltd., 1996).

him these questions: "Let me ask for further clarification on your response. If I understand you correctly, you are saying that a person who trusts in or believes in Christ and his atoning sacrifice for his sins can say that he is saved no matter how he then lives? For example, if I were to meet such a person and see that he is living in sin, and say to him that he must repent to be saved, and he responds to me that he is already saved and can't lose his salvation because he is sealed by the Holy Spirit and even though he knows he is living in sin, he is ok because he trusted Christ for salvation, then you would agree that he is saved?"

Here was his response: "Absolutely! The verses I cited show that we have forgiveness of sins through the shed blood of the Lord Jesus Christ alone. Grace and works do not mix. 'Ye are not under the law, but under grace' (Romans 6:14). 'If by grace, then is it no more of works: otherwise grace is no more grace. But if it be of works, then is it no more grace: otherwise work is no more work' (Romans 11:6). We are dead to the law (Galatians 2:19). If I start adding works, I frustrate the grace of God, making Christ's death worthless (Galatians 2:21). Also, if I start adding works, the question then becomes, how much of my salvation is due to my works and how much due to God's grace. If I avoid the 'big' sins, is that enough to keep my salvation? How about going to church every Sunday? How about giving a tithe? There are all these questions as to how much is enough to maintain my salvation. No, Ephesians 1:7 says, 'We have redemption through his blood, the forgiveness of sins, according to the riches of his grace.' How forgiven are you? According to the riches of his grace. If we have to do our part, then his grace must not be rich enough to save us. God forbid that we come to such a conclusion, because Christ's blood saved that person according to the riches of his grace. Therefore, if someone, for one second, trusts in Jesus's blood as atonement for their sins, they have eternal life. They could live the most wicked, heinous life ever known, and they would still have eternal life in heaven."

His statement, "They could live the most wicked, heinous life ever known, and they would still have eternal life in heaven" is the possible logical end conclusion of OSAS taken to the extreme.

We should note that in his answer, Eric uses some very good verses from scripture, but does not consider the whole counsel of God on the issue of salvation. One should never create a doctrine out of a few pet verses, especially when false assumptions are added.

Eric's false assumptions arise from his use of the word *works*. He uses works in a broad all-inclusive way. He makes no distinction between works of the law which cannot justify (Galatians 2:16) and works of faith which do justify (James 2:24). So let's see what scripture has to say about a Christian who is as wicked as can be in regard to eternal life.

10. In Romans 6:16, what does obedience to sin lead to?

____

11. In Titus 1:16, how do those who profess to know God, deny him? ________________________________

12. In 2 Timothy 2:12, what happens to those who deny Christ? __________________________________

13. What does 1 John 1:6–7 say about those who walk in darkness? __________________________________

____

14. In Hebrews 10:26–27, what happens to those who deliberately keep on sinning? ________________________

____

15. In 1 John 3:8, what is said about those who make a practice of sinning? ______________________________

____

16. In John 8:44, what is said of those who are of the devil?

____

____

17. In 1 John 3:9, what is said about those who are born of God? ____________________________________

____

18. In 1 John 3:10, how do we know who belongs to God and who belongs to the devil? _____________________

____

Here is Galatians 6:7–8 from the NIV: "Do not be deceived: God cannot be mocked. A man reaps what he sows. The one who sows to please his sinful nature, from that nature will reap destruction; the one who sows to please the Spirit, from the Spirit will reap eternal life."

19. What happens to those who please their sinful nature?

____

____

The OSAS doctrine contends that once you have been born again, you could conceivably live a sinful lifestyle from then on and still inherit eternal life upon your death. You could make sin a deliberate ongoing practice of your life and still be saved. We have seen from the scriptures above that those who do so are not saved but are of the devil and desire to do the devil's desires rather than God's. If you are of the devil, you most certainly are not of God. If you sow to please your sinful nature, you will reap destruction as opposed to eternal life.

Let us turn our attention now to the teachings of John Calvin.

Since Calvinism has had such an impact on Christian doctrine, let's begin by briefly considering the teachings of Calvin. His basic theology has been summed up by an acronym: TULIP.

- T—total depravity of man (Man is so depraved that he is unable to come to faith in Christ as Lord and Savior and thus spiritual birth happens before faith.)
- U—unconditional election (Calvin teaches that faith is not a condition of salvation but a consequence of your election and regeneration by God and it is only God who can and will determine who will and who will not be saved. When God regenerates you, he gives you faith to believe.)
- L—limited atonement (Christ died only for the elect and not for those whom God would not elect.)
- I – irresistible grace (God calls the elect to salvation and they cannot resist the call.)

- P – perseverance of the saints (Calvin teaches that God will make sure that you will persevere to the end; if you don't persevere, it is evidence that God never really chose you to be saved in the first place.)

T of TULIP

Let's look at what the scriptures have to say about Calvin's teaching. Under T, for total depravity, Calvin teaches that man is unable to come to faith in Christ because he is totally depraved. Yet there is not a single verse that explicitly states we are unable to come to faith in Christ. There are certainly scriptures that explicitly teach we are depraved. But there are none that explicitly state that we are unable to come to salvation as a result of our depravity. Since Calvin believes that man cannot come to faith on his own, he teaches God must unconditionally elect whomever he wishes to be saved. He elects them before the foundation of the world. Therefore, Calvin teaches that mankind has no choice in salvation. He is totally dependent on God choosing him. If God does not choose him, he will be eternally lost, and there is nothing he can do about it. By the same token, if God does choose him, he will be saved regardless, and he cannot resist God so, again, man has no choice in the matter.

I would expect that if Calvin is correct about salvation in that we have absolutely no choice or ability to believe in Christ for salvation, then there would be no instructions in the Word of God encouraging us to believe in Christ. If God is the only one making that determination, there is no need to tell us how to be saved since we are incapable of making that choice. If Calvin is right, when the Philippian jailer asked Paul what he must do to be saved, Paul's answer should have been, "Nothing, only God can save you!"

However, that is not what Paul said. In fact, in scripture, we see many admonitions for us to believe in Christ unto salvation. Some Calvinists might argue that they should share the gospel to all because we do not know who is elect and who is not. That argument is specious as it would refute Calvin's teaching that one must be saved before he believes. It does not matter if one is elect or nonelect. Calvin teaches you cannot believe until you are elect and regenerated. Therefore, there would be no point to telling someone they must believe in the Lord Jesus Christ. According to Calvin, that is an impossibility until after they are saved by God.

The following verses all tell us how to be saved. Note the order of salvation: is it believe and be saved or be saved and then believe?

In the following passages, does a person believe before or after he is saved? Check the correct answer.

20. John 1:12 _______before _______after
21. Acts 2:38 _______before _______after
22. Romans 10:9 _______before _______after
23. Acts 16:31 _______before _______after
24. Luke 7:44–50 _______before _______after
25. Mark 16:16 _______before _______after
26. Acts 2:21 _______before _______after

U of TULIP

It should be noted that in each of the above verses, a person first believes in Christ and salvation is the result. It should also be noted that there is no verse that explicitly states that man is saved before he believes on the Lord Jesus Christ. Now let us consider if faith is required of man to be saved or if he must be elected and regenerated first and then receive faith from God to believe the gospel.

27. Matthew 9:2 _______faith required _______faith not required
28. Romans 3:26 _______faith required _______faith not required
29. Romans 3:28 _______faith required _______faith not required
30. Romans 4:5 _______faith required _______faith not required
31. Romans 4:9 _______faith required _______faith not required
32. Romans 4:16 _______faith required _______faith not required

33. Romans 5:1 _______faith required _______faith not required
34. Galatians 3:24 _______faith required _______faith not required
35. Ephesians 2:8 _______faith required _______faith not required

It is clear from these verses that believing (or faith) resulted in justification unto salvation and not salvation first, resulting in faith. In fact, in the account from Luke 7:44–50, Jesus clearly states that it is the woman's faith that saved her. These verses clearly refute the notion that sinful man cannot come to faith in Christ for salvation and that he must be justified and saved first by God and then God will give him believing faith. No verse can be found that explicitly states that a person is first saved or justified before he can have faith in Christ.

Scripture does tell us how faith comes about. It never says we are given faith after God's grace saves us. That would be a case of being saved by "grace alone" instead of by faith in Christ alone. In order to be saved, we certainly need God's grace, but his grace is given as a result of our faith in Christ.

36. In Romans 5:2, how do we have access to God's grace?

   ____

37. Describe the process of how faith comes about as recorded in Romans 10:13–17.

   ____

   ____

   ____

So faith comes from hearing the Word of Christ from those sent to preach the gospel.

L of TULIP

Did Jesus die on a cross to pay the penalty for sin for everyone, or only for a few people?

38.	John 1:29	_______ all	_______ only a few
39.	John 3:16	_______ all	_______ only a few
40.	John 3:17	_______ all	_______ only a few
41.	John 4:42	_______ all	_______ only a few
42.	John 12:32	_______ all	_______ only a few
43.	Romans 8:32	_______ all	_______ only a few
44.	2 Corinthians 5:14–15	_______ all	_______ only a few
45.	1 Timothy 2:5–6	_______ all	_______ only a few
46.	1 Timothy 4:10	_______ all	_______ only a few
47.	Hebrews 2:9	_______ all	_______ only a few
48.	1 John 2:2	_______ all	_______ only a few

These verses, and many others, clearly teach that Jesus Christ died a horrific death on the cross for all people, the whole world, and for everyone. In fact, 1 John 2:2 informs us that his atoning sacrifice was not just for us, the elect, but also for the sins of the whole world. That would include the nonelect also. Jesus said in Matthew 7:14 that the gate is narrow that leads to life and only a few find it. Jesus did not die just for the few. He died that all may come to Christ for eternal life if they are willing.

These verses contradict Calvin's idea of limited atonement—that Jesus only died for the elect. For there is not a single verse in all of scripture that explicitly states that Jesus did not die for all people or that he died for only the elect or only for a few.

It should be noted that Jesus atoned for the sins of the world but did not forgive the sins of the world. He paid the penalty for sins so that through repentance and faith in Christ we might be forgiven of them. That is why we preach "repentance for the forgiveness of sins" (Luke 24:46) and faith in Christ.

I of TULIP

Can a person resist God?

49. Exodus 16:28   _______yes _______no

50. 1 Samuel 8:7   _______yes _______no

51. Jeremiah 15:6   _______yes _______no

52. Proverbs 1:24–26   _______yes _______no

53. Proverbs 21:7   _______yes _______no

54. Luke 7:29–30   _______yes _______no

55. John 5:40   _______yes _______no

56. Acts 7:51   _______yes _______no

These verses and many more all demonstrate that man can reject what God says, refuse to listen to his commands, and resist his will. Anyone can reject God and refuse to believe in Christ's sacrificial death on the cross on his behalf. There is no verse that explicitly states that man cannot resist God.

P of TULIP

Look up the following passages and decide if they indicate that a believer can or cannot be lost after justification. Make a check mark for the correct category.

57. John 10:27–30   _______can be lost _______cannot be lost

58. Romans 8:38–39   _______can be lost _______cannot be lost

59. Colossians 1:21–23   _______can be lost _______cannot be lost

60. Hebrews 10:26–27   _______can be lost _______cannot be lost

61. John 6:37–40   _______can be lost _______cannot be lost

62. Galatians 5:2–4   _______can be lost _______cannot be lost

63. Galatians 6:7–8   _______can be lost _______cannot be lost

64. Ephesians 1:13–14   _______can be lost _______cannot be lost

65. Hebrews 6:4–6 ________can be lost ________cannot be lost
66. 1ˢᵗ Corinthians 15:1–2 ________can be lost ________cannot be lost
67. John 15:5–6 ________can be lost ________cannot be lost
68. 1ˢᵗ Peter 1:3–5 ________can be lost ________cannot be lost
69. 2ⁿᵈ Peter 1:5–11 ________can be lost ________cannot be lost
70. 2ⁿᵈ Peter 2:20–22 ________can be lost ________cannot be lost
71. John 3:16 ________can be lost ________cannot be lost
72. John 5:24 ________can be lost ________cannot be lost
73. Galatians 5:19–21 ________can be lost ________cannot be lost

Which category of verses above are true? Since all scripture is God-breathed, and there are no contradictions in the Word of God, all the above verses are true.

I have written that there are no verses that explicitly state: (1) that we are unable to come to faith in Christ for salvation because of our depravity; (2) that a person is first saved or justified before we come to faith in Christ; (3) that Jesus did not die for all people; (4) that man cannot resist God; and (5) that a person can never lose eternal life after coming to a saving faith in Jesus. When I say explicit, I mean that the verse is without vagueness or ambiguity. It leaves no question as to the intent or meaning. This is in contrast to implicit, which means you imply something though it is not specifically expressed.

Each of the five points of TULIP are all drawn from scriptures through inference or assumptions from other scriptures. None of the five points are explicitly stated in scripture. Calvin comes to his conclusions by inferring or making assumptions from verses that do not explicitly state what he is concluding. In so doing, he contradicts the explicit statements in scripture to the contrary.

This does not mean that we should never infer things from scriptures that do not explicitly state what the Bible teaches. The Word of God does not explicitly state that God is a triune God or that there is a trinity. We infer the trinity from examining scriptures that would otherwise be contradictory if there were no trinity. We cannot do this with the concepts of TULIP since as we have seen, there are many verses that explicitly contradict the assumptions that form TULIP. If we infer things from scripture that cannot be confirmed by other scriptures, but rather contradict them, we should give pause to reconsider what we are inferring.

Calvin's theology all flows from a false presupposition. He starts with the biblical teaching of total depravity. The scriptures clearly teach that man is depraved. There is no one that does good. We all like sheep have turned away and gone astray. None are righteous and no one seeks God. The heart is desperately wicked. And there are many other assertions that expose our sinful state. I don't know of any Christian teacher that would disagree with the idea that we are depraved, nor do I.

The problem with Calvin's teaching on depravity is that he takes it too far and says we are so totally depraved that we cannot, indeed, are unable to come to faith in Christ for salvation. From this false presupposition flows the rest of his theology. For if man cannot even believe that Jesus is the Son of God and that he died for us and rose from the dead and decide to turn from his sin, how can he be saved? He is completely helpless and can do nothing to be saved. Therefore, he must be saved some other way than by faith in Christ. God would then be the only being who could save you. If God chooses not to save you, you are doomed to hell with nothing you can do to prevent going there. What a horrible thing to consider. What a horrible thing to think that God would doom most people to enter the wide gate that leads to destruction and only choose a few people to enter the narrow gate that leads to life.

If we conclude that man is incapable of choosing to believe in Christ for salvation, then it logically makes sense that God would be the only one who determines who will or will not be saved. If God is the only one who determines who will be saved, then we can logically conclude that Jesus only died for those people. If we conclude that Jesus died only for those God chose, we could then conclude that those God did choose for salvation cannot resist his will to be saved. Then of course, we could conclude that God will make sure a person will persevere to the end and never lose out on eternal life. Can you see how the U, L, I, and P of TULIP naturally flows from the T? The whole system stems from a false presupposition.

The scriptures teach there are two basic ways to forfeit your eternal life. One is through going back to obeying the law as a means of justification and the other is to go back to a life of sin.

In the churches of Galatia, there were Judaizers that were teaching that you still had to keep the law for justification. Paul dismisses that argument in Galatians 5:4. He says, "You are severed from Christ, you who would be justified by the law; you have fallen away from grace." Recall from 2 Corinthians 13:5 that Christ is in you unless you are disqualified. Here in Galatians Paul states that going back to keeping the law results in you being severed from Christ. If you are severed from Christ, Christ is no longer in you, and you are disqualified. In 1 John 5:11–12, it states, "And this is the testimony, that God gave us eternal life, and this life is in his Son. Whoever has the Son has life; whoever does not have the Son of God does not have life." I think it should be plain to all that if you go back to keeping the law, you will be severed from Christ and will no longer have eternal life because you are no longer in Christ. You have been severed from him.

The other way to forfeit your eternal life is to go back to a life of sin. Consider Hebrews 10:26–29, "If we deliberately keep on sinning after we have received the knowledge of the truth, no sacrifice for sins is left, but only a fearful expectation of judgment and of raging fire that will consume the enemies of God. Anyone who rejected the law of Moses died without mercy on the testimony of two or three witnesses. How much more severely do you think a man deserves to be punished who has trampled the Son of God under foot, who has treated as an unholy thing the blood of the covenant that sanctified him, and who has insulted the Spirit of grace?" (NIV).

Notice that this passage speaks of those who have received the knowledge of the truth (v. 26) and have been sanctified by the blood of the covenant (v. 29). If they should deliberately continue to live in sin, they will not enjoy eternal life but face judgment and raging fire that will consume the enemies of God.

The warning from Hebrews 10:26 against a continuous lifestyle of sin is expressed in other passages as well. Consider Galatians 5:19–21. After listing a host of sins, Paul states that if you live like this, you will not inherit the kingdom. In 1 John 3:8, it is also instructive: "Whoever makes a practice of sinning is of the devil, for the devil has been sinning from the beginning. The reason the Son of God appeared was to destroy the works of the devil."

Most people who believe in OSAS ignore passages to the contrary. If confronted with them, they try really hard to explain them away to avoid what is being said. Those who believe in Calvin's perseverance of the saints have a really slick way of dealing with it. They just negate the person's salvation and say they were never saved in the first place. I will share more about that in the next lesson on assurance of salvation.

Since there are verses that teach both eternal security and forfeiture of eternal life, how do we reconcile both sets of verses without denying the truth of either of them? It is really very simple.

Let me explain. We have two very similar promises in the gospel of John. In John 14:14, Jesus says, "If you ask me anything in my name, I will do it." And in John 16:23, Jesus says, "In that day you will ask nothing of me. Truly, truly, I say to you, whatever you ask of the Father in my name, he will give it to you." The promises are given that if you ask either Jesus or the Father for anything in Jesus's name, it will be given to you.

Have you received everything you have asked for in the name of Jesus? I doubt anyone has. The reason is because there are lots of verses on prayer that give conditions for receiving what you ask for. The promises Jesus has given are conditional promises. One such condition is that you will not receive what you ask for if you are asking out of selfish motives. Here is James 4:3, "When you ask, you do not receive, because you ask with wrong motives, that you may spend what you get on your pleasures" (NIV). You may conclude from James that even if you are asking for something in Jesus's name, you will not receive it when you ask with wrong motives. James puts a condition on answered prayer. This demonstrates that God does not list every condition (or sometimes any conditions at all) when he makes a promise. We must study to find and understand the conditions to correctly understand the word of truth.

To sum up, the promises given guaranteeing salvation, eternal life, and passing from death to life are conditional. The conditions that would negate the promise are found in the opposing set of verses. We have previously taught that salvation is a lifelong endeavor. We were saved (justified), we are being saved (sanctified), and we will be saved (glorified). Jesus said that those who endure to the end will be saved. Do not succumb to anything that could cause you to fall away before you have reached glorification.

Let me give you a couple demonstrations of how salvation is conditional based on a verse that gives the condition within the verse. Typical conditional statements often use if-then syntax. These statements will have a condition, the *if* part and a result, the *then* part. For example, one might say, "If it is cloudy on Saturday, then I will not go to the beach." The condition is "if it is cloudy on Saturday" and the result is "I will not go to the beach." This is usually shortened by eliminating the word *then* so that it reads, "If it is cloudy on Saturday, I will not go to the beach." We could even change the order of the if-then statements. We could say, "I will not go to the beach if it is cloudy on Saturday." We see this type of syntax in passages dealing with salvation. Here is one example from 1 Corinthians 15:2, "And by which you are being saved, if you hold fast to the word I preached to you—unless you believed in vain."

74. What is the "if" part of the verse? _______________________
75. What is the "then" part of the verse? _______________________
76. In the last phrase of 1 Corinthians 15:2, what is the result of not holding firmly to the Word preached to you?

____

Another example is found in Colossians 1:21–23, "Once you were alienated from God and were enemies in your minds because of your evil behavior. But now he has reconciled you by Christ's physical body through death to present you holy in his sight, without blemish and free from accusation—if you continue in your faith, established and firm, not moved from the hope held out in the gospel. This is the gospel that you heard and that has been proclaimed to every creature under heaven, and of which I, Paul, have become a servant."

77. What is the "if" part in verse 23? _______________________
78. What is the then part in verses 21-22? _______________________

1 Corinthians 15 and Colossians 1 are two examples that place conditions upon whether we finish the race or not.

If we understand that God's promises concerning eternal life are conditioned upon our completing the race, then there are no contradictions with the verses proclaiming we have eternal life and those that proclaim that we could forfeit eternal life. This understanding of the passages confirms that our salvation is not fully accomplished by a single moment in time when we come to faith in Christ, but rather by completing the race and enduring to the end.

In conclusion, if we contend that salvation passages are unconditional promises that are absolute and can never be broken, we end up with a lot of contradictions in the Word. However, if we understand that those passages about salvation and eternal life are conditional and reliant upon other scriptures that amplify and clarify them, then they are still true and there are no contradictions.

Why is all this so important? Think about what the end would be if you took the once saved, always saved belief to its logical conclusion. If you took it to the extreme, you would have to accept that a saved person could fall into sin and live in blatant intentional and unrepentant sin all his life after conversion but would still have eternal life. This is nothing less than giving someone a license to sin. Jude has strong words about such a belief. In verse 4, he says, "For certain men whose condemnation was written about long ago have secretly slipped in among you. They are godless men, who change the grace of our God into a license for immorality and deny Jesus Christ our only Sovereign and Lord" (NIV). And don't forget 1 John 3:8 which was quoted earlier: "If you make a practice of sinning, you are of the devil!" A person cannot be both of the devil and of Jesus Christ at the same time.

Hopefully, it is clear that the importance of a proper understanding of what scripture teaches about eternal security should keep one from falling away from the faith. A proper understanding should also keep one from becoming lukewarm in their faith. Perhaps this is why Paul taught the believers to "continue in the faith" as found in Acts 14:21–22!

ASSURANCE OF SALVATION

The issue of knowing for sure that a person is saved and will inherit eternal life has been troublesome for many Christians. This is a healthy concern. A person should examine their life to make sure they are on the narrow road that leads to life. Indeed, Paul even wrote to the Corinthians that they should examine themselves to see if they are in the faith. It should be noted that if the Christians in Corinth could never "lose" their salvation, as some teach, then Paul's admonition to examine themselves to see if they are in the faith would be pointless. If you can't "lose" salvation, then by default, you would still be in the faith. Why would you test yourself to see if you were still in the faith, if you cannot fall away?

God does not leave us to wonder without assurance. John penned 1 John for the express purpose that you may know you have eternal life. Here is what he wrote in 1 John 5:13, "I write these things to you who believe in the name of the Son of God, that you may know that you have eternal life." We will take a look at what this short book has to say to us about our assurance.

1. What does 1ˢᵗ John 5:1 say about those who believe that Jesus is the Christ? _______________________________

____

Being born of God is a spiritual birth. We have all been born physically, which is your first birth. Being born of God is your spiritual birth or second birth. This is where the term *born again* comes from. John 1:12 tells us that being born of God comes about by receiving Jesus Christ and believing in his name. If you have been born of God, you have eternal life. It is fitting that John should include believing that Jesus is the Christ as an assurance that a person has eternal life since believing in Jesus is what originally justifies us. The rest of the assurances we have are all based on things that we do.

2.   What do we learn from 1 John 1:6–7? _______________

____

____

3.   How can we be sure of our salvation according to 1 John 2:3–5? _______________

____

4.   In John 14:21, what did Jesus say about those who love him?

____

____

The context of 1 John 2:3–5 is about Jesus. We have learned that we cannot be saved by works of the law. Then how is it that we can know we have eternal life by obeying the commands of Jesus? It is because we are not obeying his commands in an attempt to be saved and thus have something to boast about. Rather, we obey his commands out of love for him. We do so by faith in appreciation of what he has done for us. If we do not make at least an attempt to obey his commands, we would have a legitimate reason to question what is in our heart and the status of our salvation.

5.   What is the lesson from 1 John 2:9–11? _______________

____

6.   What does the gospel of John 3:19–21 say about light and darkness? _______________

____

7. 1 John 3:14–15 expands upon what we learned in question 5. What does John add in this passage? _______________

____

8. Who is it that lives forever according to 1 John 2:17?

____

9. Who is it that has eternal life according to 1 John 2:24–25?

____

In the gospel of John, in chapter 15, Jesus stressed the importance of remaining (or abiding) in him. If you remain in him, you will produce fruit. If you are in Christ and do not bear fruit, you are taken away, cut off or removed (verse 2) and gathered, thrown away, and burned in the fire (verse 6). Therefore, it is important that you remember what you have heard in the beginning, for if you do, you will remain in the Son. What you heard in the beginning should be along the lines of salvation by grace through faith and not of works of the law. It comes by repentance from sin and being born again. It is believing in Christ and confessing him as Lord. It is the death, burial, and resurrection of our Lord.

10. What do we learn from 1 John 3:6? _______________

____

This passage really highlights the importance of repentance. When you come to faith in Christ, if there is no desire to turn from your sins, but rather you continue on in them, scripture declares that you have neither seen nor known Christ. This is in direct contradiction to the Free Grace movement, which teaches that repentance is not necessary for salvation. Astonishingly, I have even heard a message teaching that if you repent of your sins, you will go to hell! This comes from the false definition that says repentance is only a change of mind and not a turning from sin because of a change of mind.

In Luke 13:6–9, Jesus tells a parable about a fig tree that did not bear fruit for three years. The man who planted it was going to have it cut down, but the one who was taking care of the vineyard asked to have it remain for another year so that he could dig around it and fertilize it. Then if it didn't bear fruit, it could be cut down.

I am not saying that God gives you a total of four years to begin to bear fruit or repent of your sins. What I do conclude from Jesus's parable is that God is very gracious and patient and waits to see if you will bear fruit. This also brings to mind the Parable of the Sower found in Luke 8:4–15. The seed that fell on the rocky soil springs up quickly but has no root so bears no fruit. The seed that fell among the thorns apparently produced some fruit, but it did not mature.

I am concerned that in America today, there are many people who are called to Christ and pray a "prayer of salvation" but do not understand what is really involved. I have heard many calls to come to Christ, but repentance is scarcely ever mentioned. There is no explanation of what God expects of those who come to him. Many times, people are encouraged to come to Christ, and he will fix their loneliness or depression or lack of purpose. The focus seems to be more on what Christ can do for you than it is on what God desires for your life. God may indeed fix all those things because he loves you, but it comes through repentance from sin. It comes from turning from darkness to light. It comes from living a life to please him rather than yourself. Sin is the root cause of most of man's problems. God knows this and can help you overcome the sin in your life.

11. In 1 John 3:8–10, how do we know who are God's children and who are of the devil? ___________________________

____

____

____

This passage is a powerful statement about the practice of sin in a believer's life. Anyone who is in Christ is a new creation. He does not continue in a life of sin. In fact, Hebrews 10:26–30 states that the believer who deliberately keeps on sinning will only have raging fire that consumes the enemies of God to look forward to. In this instance, there is no longer any sacrifice for his sin.

We see again the dual nature of our relationship with God found in Philippians 2:12–13. We are to work out our salvation. This means we are to deal with the sin in our life. We are to become more like Christ as we walk with him. And it is God who works in us to help us bear fruit and do and act as he wants us to.

Verse 9 mentions the reason why we cannot go on sinning. It is because God's seed remains in us. Galatians 3:16 refers to promises given to Abraham and to his "seed." This seed is identified as being Christ. So as long as Christ remains in you and you remain in Christ, you will not make a practice of sinning. Jesus commands us in John 15:4 to remain in him. If you do, then he says he will remain in you. Christ is faithful and will remain in you so long as you remain in him. It is only you who can choose to not remain in Christ. Remember from John 15 that if you are in Christ but do not produce fruit, you will be taken away and thrown into the fire.

12. How do we know that we belong to the truth in 1 John 3:16–20? _______________________________________

____

13. What two things assure us that we live in God according to 1 John 4:12–13?

    a. ____

    a. ____

How can one know that the Holy Spirit is really living in him? The Spirit's presence is not something we can feel or detect by our five senses. Probably the best way to know is by seeing the fruit of the Spirit becoming more evident in our lives. There are nine qualities mentioned in Galatians 5:22–23 that are said to be fruit of the Spirit. The longer a person walks with the Lord, the more evidence there should be of the Spirit's fruit. Another indicator that the Spirit is living in you is whether or not you are seeking the Lord. At the end of lesson 3, you were asked to set a time aside each day for daily devotions. Romans 3:11 says of the lost that no one seeks God. If you are seeking God by worshipping him and praying to him, you are doing something the Apostle Paul says that the lost do not do! Perhaps that is good evidence of the Spirit in your life also!

And finally:

14. Who has eternal life according to 1 John 5:11–12? ________

____

When we consider all the things John said that would help us to know that we have eternal life, we find that most of what he teaches us is based on what we do. That includes things such as loving our brothers, walking in the light, obeying God's commands, etc.

Yes, all those things are works, but not works of the law. They are works of faith which are done by faith out of love for God. They are necessary evidence that tell us that we indeed have eternal life. Don't fall into the trap of wondering if you have done enough works to "maintain" your salvation. Doing works to get saved or maintain a person's salvation are works of the law, which cannot save. They are works that you can boast about but do nothing as far as salvation is concerned. When a person has been born again, he will obey God's commands because he loves God and wants to please him. That obedience gives no justification for boasting. We know that we have eternal life because we are in Christ. As 1 John 5:12 says, "Whoever has the Son has life."

Salvation is not dependent on how many works we do. The important thing is that you are walking with the Lord and are producing fruit. Jesus promised us that if we remain or abide in him, we will bear much fruit. John 15:5 says, "I am the vine; you are the branches. Whoever abides in me and I in him, he it is that bears much fruit, for apart from me you can do nothing." Strive to love God with all your heart and you will bear much fruit.

Before leaving the subject of assurance of salvation, it is important to note that there can be no assurance of salvation under John Calvin's theology. If you recall, his theology teaches that God is the only one who determines who will be saved. There is no way for a person to know for sure if they truly are one of the chosen. Someone who believes they are chosen may be able to point to many of the assurances of eternal life that John gives. That, however, does not provide any assurance of salvation for the Calvinist. For Calvin teaches that those evidence might only be an "inferior operation of the Spirit." In the end, you will be cast off as one of the reprobates. If a person doesn't persevere, they will be condemned as never having been saved in the first place.

Robert Shank addresses this issue. He starts by quoting Calvin:

> In all these passages and others that could be cited, the warnings are directed toward men who obviously are conceived of as being members of the elect body, the true ekklesia. Unless the words of Christ and his Apostles are to be dismissed as mere rhetorical hypothesis, without foundation in fact, or unless we accept Calvin's assumption (3:2:11,12) of an "inferior operation of the Spirit" by which he enlightens some with a present sense of grace which afterwards proves "evanescent" and "sheds some rays of grace on the reprobate, afterwards allowing these to be extinguished" so that by the express design of God, they perish—all because "the will of God is immutable" and his eternal counsel for them was reprobation rather than salvation, so that "when God shows himself propitious to them, it is not as if he had truly rescued them from death and taken them under his protection," despite the fact that they "believe God to be propitious to them, inasmuch as they accept the gift of reconciliation"…ad infinitum, ad nauseam (God plays games with the souls of men? The death of Christ for the sins of the whole world was all in fun?)… unless we can accept such horrible assumptions,

we must recognize that the bible affirms the reality of the apostasy of members of the elect body.[6]

It makes perfect sense under Calvinism to say that one who falls away was never truly saved to begin with. For if God is the only determiner of salvation, and he can cause some to think that they were saved when they were not, and then allowed them to be lost, one can only conclude that they were never really chosen by God. Therefore, under Calvinism, unless you can predict your own future, there is absolutely no way to have assurance of salvation until you die. For you cannot know for sure whether or not God genuinely saved you or was only propitious toward you and you are one of the reprobates that he will cast off in the end. By then, it is too late.

Fortunately, we can know that we are saved because we do what the scriptures instruct us to do. We repented of our sins, placed our faith in Jesus to save us, and were baptized. Subsequently, we walk in the Spirit and have all the assurances that John gives us in 1 John. We continue to live in him, being sanctified day by day, until one day we will be glorified! Beloved, keep the faith!

---

[6] Robert Shank, *Elect in the Son: A Study of the Doctrine of Election*, p. 53 (Springfield, Missouri: Bethany House Publishers, 1970).

The Rapture of the Church

I would be remiss if I did not finish this course on growing in Christ and not address what I consider to be the second most wide-spread false teaching being taught today—the teaching of a pretribulation rapture. The first most widespread false teaching is believing that upon the moment of salvation, your salvation is complete.

Before I begin this topic, I would ask you to think back in your own life. If you believe that the rapture will happen before the tribulation, did you come to that conclusion because you were taught it by others? Did you hear the sermons, watch the movies, read the books, and see the videos all teaching a pretribulation rapture? Or did you come to believe in it strictly from what scripture teaches? When you read and studied scripture, were you influenced by ideas taught by those believing in a pretribulation rapture? If much of your belief has come from what you have been taught, rather than what you discovered on your own through scripture, I would ask you to take a fresh look at it. Seriously consider what the scriptures have to say.

In 1 Timothy 4:1, it states that in later times some will depart from the faith. I am concerned that there will be many who believe in a pretribulation rapture that will be among those who fall away from the faith. When the events of Revelation play out, the Antichrist will appear and require all to take a mark on their right hand or on their forehead. Without that mark, no one will be able to buy or sell things without it. When people who have been taught all their life that they will be taken up in a rapture before this time find themselves facing the Antichrist, they will be confused and may feel betrayed by those who taught them all their lives that they would not be here at that time. Couple that with having been taught that they cannot lose eternal life under any circumstances, and you have a very dangerous prospect. Out of confusion and fear that they cannot buy food without the Antichrist's mark, they may fall away and take the mark. There is no coming back from that.

Personally, I had believed in a pretribulation rapture for over forty years of my life. I had read books, heard sermons, and saw the movies that all taught a rapture happening before the tribulation begins. The one thing I did not do was to study the scriptures by themselves to test whether I had been taught correctly.

Then one day I was leading a small home Bible study, and those attending wanted to study the end times. I decided that I would only use the Bible and a concordance to study the events leading up to the return of Christ. I did not consult other authors or commentaries or watch any videos on the topic. I just used the Bible. What happened was I came away with a new perspective on the issue. It was very hard for me to change my beliefs on the pretribulation rapture for I had believed in one for such a long time. But I could not deny what the scriptures were actually teaching me.

I never thought it really necessary to study the issue because the way I saw it was if someone believed in a midtribulation or posttribulation rapture, they would simply be taken up to meet the Lord in the clouds earlier than they expected. So there would be no harm, no foul. In other words, if believers are taken up earlier than expected, there was no danger to them. Once I realized there would be no early escape from the trial coming upon the earth, I became concerned for those who are as deceived as I once was about the timing of the rapture. Therefore, this lesson is for all who still believe in a pretribulation rapture. Many entire books have been written on the subject.

Therefore, I will try to cut through all of issues quickly and boil it down to simple terms.

First, we must understand the basic ideas behind a pretribulation rapture. It seems most people agree that there will be a seven-year period of tribulation immediately preceding the return of Christ. This comes from Daniel 9. Daniel 9 teaches that seventy weeks (of years) was decreed for the Jews. Sixty-nine of them have been fulfilled leaving one week (seven years) remaining prior to the return of the Lord. It also seems everyone agrees that all believers will be taken up to meet the Lord in the clouds before his return. What is not in agreement is the timing of this event which has been called the rapture of the church.

Here are the basic tenets of a pretribulation rapture:

1. The Lord's return is imminent (which means it could happen at any time without any prophesied events that must happen before his return).
2. All believers will be raptured prior to the beginning of the seven-year tribulation (they will be taken up into the clouds to meet the Lord in the air).
3. It is a signless event (there are no indications of exactly when it would happen).
4. It will be a silent and secret coming.
5. The Lord will return in the clouds, will rapture the church, and then return to heaven.
6. The third coming of the Lord will be seven years later (it is not referred to as a third coming since none is mentioned in scripture, but essentially, that is what it would be).
7. Believers are not destined for wrath.
8. Only believers see Christ in a pretribulation rapture.

The first thing that we should note is that there is no mention in scripture of a second and third coming of the Lord. Scripture only speaks of the Lord's return. It is said that the pretribulation rapture and second coming are two phases of Christ's second coming. This is another wild assumption made to try and justify a false doctrine.

If there is a pretribulation rapture as described and a second coming as foretold in scripture, how could they be two phases of the same return? If Jesus comes once and gathers the believers to himself in the clouds and then years later comes back to gather the rest of his believers in the clouds, how is that not two separate comings of Jesus?

The second thing to note is that there are no verses anywhere that explicitly state or teach any of the eight points above. The one exception would be that believers are not destined for wrath. That is explicitly stated and is true but usually in the context of wrath resulting in eternal damnation. We are not appointed to wrath of that kind but rather to eternal life. The argument is made though that believers will escape the tribulation because God is pouring his wrath out at that time. Then I would argue that there will still be believers in the tribulation. Why do they have to endure this time of wrath? Are we more special believers than they are? If there are no believers that will experience the wrath of God being poured out during the tribulation, then one must of necessity conclude that there will be no saints at that time. It is clear from the book of Revelation there are saints during the tribulation.

The third thing we can note is that since there are no verses that explicitly teach a pretribulation rapture, then the whole doctrine is made from speculation, assumptions, and inferences taken from various verses. A classic example of this is from 1 Thessalonians 4:13–17. It is taught from this passage that Jesus comes back, raptures the dead along with the believers that remain on earth at that time, and then returns to heaven with them. Nowhere does it say that Jesus returns to heaven at this time. It is assumed in order to teach a pretribulation rapture. It is fine to draw inferences from scripture as long as you find scriptural support from other passages as well. However, there is zero scriptural support for the idea that Jesus returns to earth in the clouds and then turns right around and goes back to heaven. In all passages describing Christ's second coming, none of them teach that he immediately returns to heaven. Rather, many of them describe his coming down to earth and beginning his thousand-year reign.

Much ballyhoo has been made of the idea that Jesus could come back at any moment. The fourth thing we should note is that the entire doctrine for a pretribulation rapture hinges on whether or not his coming is imminent. For if there are things that must take place before he returns, then his return cannot be imminent. Those prophesied events must take place for prophecy to be fulfilled. It is at this very point that the entire pretribulation doctrine falls apart.

In Matthew 24:3, the disciples asked Jesus, "What will be the sign of your coming and of the end of the age?" Jesus taught them that many things must take place before his return. He said that many would come claiming to be the Christ, there would be wars and rumors of wars, and there would be famines and earthquakes in various places. These are just the beginning of birth pains! Then Jesus describes a great number of other things that will take place before his return. One of those things is the rise of the Antichrist. This agrees with what is said in 2 Thessalonians 2:1–4.

So Jesus taught that many things must happen before he returns. In other words, his return would not be imminent. He did not teach he would return twice. This alone should be enough to dispense with the idea of a pretribulation rapture because Christ's return cannot happen until the prophesied events take place.

Ed Hindson and Mark Hitchcock wrote an entire book that teaches a pretribulation rapture. In that book, they make this statement: "A fourth argument against the imminency of the rapture is that it is not explicitly taught in Scripture. While it is true no single verse alone specifically says Jesus is coming to rapture his saints before the seven-year Tribulation…"[7]

I left off the last part of that sentence because that is where they put forth their assumptions as to why they think it is necessary for there to be a rapture before the tribulation. I don't subscribe to man's assumptions unless there is solid scriptural support for them which do not contradict explicit statements to the contrary. We will see that is exactly what happens.

Let's take a look at what scripture does teach on this subject. In Acts 1:6–11, Jesus left his disciples and ascended into heaven

---

[7] Ed Hinson and Mark Hitchcock, *Can We Still Believe in the Rapture?*, p. 128 (Eugene, Oregon: Harvest House Publishers, 2017).

in a cloud. Two men in white robes appeared and told the disciples that Jesus would come in the same way as he went—that is, in a cloud. There are only six references in the New Testament that speak of Jesus coming back in the clouds. They are Matthew 24:30, Matthew 26:24, Mark 13:26, Mark 14:62, 1 Thessalonians 4:17, and Revelation 1:7. Matthew 26:24 and Mark 14:62 both refer to when Jesus was standing before the high priest. He told them that they would see him coming in the clouds. Those verses make no reference to any other specifics concerning his return.

Revelation 1:7 mentions that when Jesus comes in the clouds, every eye will see him. This contradicts the idea that when Jesus comes in the clouds, it will be a secret coming in which only believers will see.

This leaves only three references referring to believers meeting Jesus in the clouds at his return: Matthew 24:30, Mark 13:26, and 1 Thessalonians 4:17. These three passages describe an event that we call the rapture. The word *rapture* does not appear in scripture. It is a term we use to describe what happens at Christ's return. It refers to all believers, both living and dead, meeting the Lord in the clouds at his return. In 1 Corinthians 15:50–53, it is also considered a "rapture" passage since it describes the dead being raised along with those believers who are currently alive. At that time, we will all receive an imperishable body in the twinkling of an eye. Receiving an imperishable body will be a necessity if we are going to be taken up into the clouds to meet the Lord. Our current bodies are not capable of flying!

Of the three passages that speak of believers being gathered to the Lord in the clouds, two of them explicitly state that this event will happen after the great tribulation spoken of by Jesus. Those are Matthew 24:29–31 and Mark 13:24–27. Both passages speak of Jesus returning in the clouds and gathering the elect from "the ends of the earth to the ends of heaven" (Mark 13:27).

Jesus spoke those words before the New Testament was written. No one had ever heard of a rapture and no Old Testament passage even hinted at one coming before the greatest tribulation that would ever be.

As I mentioned earlier, there are no verses that explicitly teach that we will be taken up into the clouds to meet the Lord in the air prior to the tribulation. If there was one, it would contradict the passages that where Jesus explicitly states that our gathering would happen after the tribulation.

Although the timing of the 1 Corinthian and 1 Thessalonian passages is not explicitly stated, it can be inferred from the fact that both mention that the dead are raised during this event. The scriptures are clear that the first resurrection—the resurrection of the righteous—occurs after the tribulation.

Here is Revelation 20:4–6: "Then I saw thrones, and seated on them were those to whom the authority to judge was committed. Also I saw the souls of those who had been beheaded for the testimony of Jesus and for the word of God, and those who had not worshiped the beast or its image and had not received its mark on their foreheads or their hands. They came to life and reigned with Christ for a thousand years. The rest of the dead did not come to life until the thousand years were ended. This is the first resurrection. Blessed and holy is the one who shares in the first resurrection! Over such the second death has no power, but they will be priests of God and of Christ, and they will reign with him for a thousand years."

It is clear from this passage that the first resurrection occurs after the tribulation since it includes those who were in the tribulation as having faced the beast and refused to accept his mark and are now being raised in the first resurrection. In 1 Thessalonians, it specifically states that we cannot precede the dead being raised. We cannot be raptured seven years before the dead are.

Jesus explicitly taught that he would return in the clouds and gather the elect to himself at his return *after* the great tribulation. This is when he gathers his elect—from the ends of the earth to the ends of the heavens (Mark 13:27). Where is the verse that says the elect meet Jesus in the clouds before the tribulation? There is none.

Although there are lots of other arguments for a pretribulation gathering of the saints in the clouds at Christ's return, they all become moot if Christ's return is not imminent. However, I would like to expose just one more false narrative concerning the idea that the rapture must happen before the tribulation.

In their book, Hindson and Hitchcock write: "Again, the apostle Paul addressed the coming of Christ in his first letter to the Thessalonian believers. The four criteria are noted including Christ returning at any moment. First, the 'day' will come quickly, like a 'thief.' Just as a thief arrives unexpectedly, so the rapture will take place at an unknown future time."[8]

Notice in this quote that Hindson and Hitchcock are implying that the return of Christ is imminent. They refer to his coming as "at any moment." They also tie the "coming like a thief" to the rapture. Then they equate Christ's coming with what is said in 1 Thessalonians 5:2 which says, "For you yourselves are fully aware that the day of the Lord will come like a thief in the night." So they tie the "coming like a thief" to the rapture.

Apparently, it does not occur to Hindson and Hitchcock that the day of the Lord coming as a thief in the night only applies to unbelievers. That day will surprise them. It will not surprise believers as verses 3 and 4 of the same chapter point out: "While people are saying, 'There is peace and security,' then sudden destruction will come upon them as labor pains come upon a pregnant woman, and they will not escape. But you are not in darkness, brothers, for that day to surprise you like a thief."

Two other things should be noted about the "day of the Lord" mentioned in verse 2. First, in 2 Thessalonians 2:1–4, just as Jesus taught in Matthew 24, Paul clearly teaches that the day of the Lord will not happen until the Antichrist is revealed. This clearly refutes the idea that the rapture could be imminent.

Those who believe in a pretribulation rapture have no idea when it will happen. Since it is said to be a signless event, and there is no indication when it will happen, it could be today, tomorrow, ten years from now, twenty years from now, or a hundred years from now. In other words, it puts them into the exact same camp as those who live in darkness. They would not be children of light because

---

[8]   Hinson and Hitchcock, *Can We Still Believe in the Rapture?* p. 132.

they would be "surprised" by the Lord's coming. In 1 Thessalonians, it says believers are children of light and that day *will not surprise* us as a thief in the night. Believers now have all the signs given by Jesus, the signs given by Paul and the signs given by John in the Book of Revelation to inform us of the future nearness of the Lord's coming.

Furthermore, we are told exactly when this "coming as a thief in the night" event will take place. In Revelation 16, just before the pouring out of the seventh and final bowl of God's wrath, we see that the kings of the whole world are gathered for battle at Armageddon. This is when Jesus is coming like a thief. Here is the relevant passage from Revelation 16:14–16: "For they are demonic spirits, performing signs, who go abroad to the kings of the whole world, to assemble them for battle on the great day of God the Almighty. ("Behold, I am coming like a thief! Blessed is the one who stays awake, keeping his garments on, that he may not go about naked and be seen exposed!") And they assembled them at the place that in Hebrew is called Armageddon."

This "coming as a thief" happens at Armageddon at the return of Christ! Unbelievers will still be in darkness and surprised at the Lord's coming. Believers will not be surprised at this time because they will have seen all the events in Revelation played out and know that the return is very near.

Let me sum all of this up in simple terms. Jesus taught that many things (signs) must happen before his return. He taught that at his return, all his elect from the ends of the earth to the ends of the heavens will be gathered when he returns in the clouds. He also explicitly stated that these events would happen after the events of the greatest tribulation that has or ever will be.

Many have come up with a host of verses they assume indicate a pretribulation rapture. When their assumptions directly contradict explicit statements to the contrary, they are in error. I could spend much time refuting the faulty logic accompanying a pretribulation rapture. In that case, I would have to write an entire book! However, I believe that if you open your mind to the possibility of the rapture occurring at Christ's return and continue to study the scriptures, the

Holy Spirit will guide you into all truth. You will begin to see more and more how the end time events actually play out and will be able to refute all false narratives about a pretribulation rapture. I trust the Holy Spirit will guide you into all truth as you have an open mind.

During the course of this study, I have exposed two primary doctrines that are widely taught in many churches today. I have shared that the five points of Calvin's TULIP are not explicitly taught anywhere in scripture. The entire teaching is built on assumptions and inferences from scriptures that don't explicitly state what has been concluded from them. Likewise, the doctrine of a pretribulation rapture is also almost exclusively created from making assumptions and inferences from scriptures that don't explicitly state what has been concluded from them.

I am not saying that making inferences from scripture is invalid. The doctrine of the trinity is one example of making inferences from scripture. There is no verse that states that God is a triune God or that God is a trinity or that God consists of three persons. However, when we infer those things not explicitly stated in scripture concerning a trinity, we are resolving the apparent contradictions in scripture that teach that the Father and the Son are both God. We are making clear a doctrine that resolves issues that are paradoxical. There are many things in scripture that are a paradox. A paradox is a seeming contradiction. We need to understand and explain how a paradox is not a contradiction. In other words, we resolve apparent contradictions by inferring things from scripture. Inferences made from scripture to teach a pretribulation rapture do not resolve apparent contradictions. Rather, they create contradictions that cannot be resolved. For this reason, we must reject the assumptions made from scripture to teach a pretribulation rapture.

Calvinism and the pretribulation teachings both create contradictions rather than resolve paradoxes. It is unwise to make inferences from certain scriptures that directly contradict the explicit teaching of other scriptures.

I pray that you will grow in the grace and knowledge of our Lord and Savior Jesus Christ. May God richly bless you in your study of his Word!

ANSWER KEY

All answers are taken from the ESV unless otherwise noted.

Lesson 1

1. (a) eternal punishment; (b) eternal life
2. Sin
3. Death, eternal life in Christ Jesus
4. Jesus
5. The Son of God
6. Repentance toward God and of faith in our Lord Jesus Christ
7. They should repent and turn to God, performing deeds in keeping with their repentance.
8. Repent, therefore, and turn back, that your sins may be blotted out.
9. Proclaimed a baptism of repentance for the forgiveness of sins
10. Repent and believe in the gospel.
11. They proclaimed that people should repent.
12. He commands all people everywhere to repent.
13. (a–d) Believe in Christ Jesus.
14. (a) Abraham was counted righteous by faith; (b) we are saved through faith.
15. By faith
16. The humble
17. Be born again.

18. Be born of water and the Spirit.
19. The path, the rock, thorns, good soil
20. It's impossible to be brought back to repentance if you fall away.
21. Consider trials as pure joy (NIV).
22. To test your faith to see if it is genuine
23. Add goodness, knowledge, self-control, perseverance, godliness, brotherly kindness, and love to your faith (NIV).
24. By rejoicing in the Lord, be gentle to all, do not be anxious about anything, pray with thanksgiving (NIV).
25. Cast all your anxieties on God.
26. Do not love the world or anything in it such as the desires of the flesh and of the eyes and the pride of life.
27. Your personal answer

Lesson 2

1. Past
2. Present
3. Past
4. Future
5. Present
6. Future
7. Present
8. Present
9. Future
10. You will receive the Holy Spirit (and your sins will be forgiven).
11. Whoever believes and is baptized
12. Whoever does not believe
13. Make disciples of all nations and baptize them in the name of the Father, Son, and Holy Spirit.
14. Baptism saves you through the resurrection of Jesus Christ.
15. Death
16. They have put on Christ.
17. Before

18. Good works
19. Evil works
20. Works of God
21. Works of the law
22. Dead works
23. Works of the flesh
24. Works of faith
25. Works of the law
26. You cannot be justified by works of the law.
27. We are justified by God's grace as a gift.
28. By faith apart from works of the law
29. The law of faith
30. Abraham was made righteous because he believed God.
31. Abraham was justified by works.
32. His faith
33. Abraham believed God.
34. Abraham offered his son by faith.
35. Works of faith
36. A person is justified by works and not by faith alone. These are works of faith.
37. Faith that has not works is dead.

Lesson 3

1. Answers will vary—a good start would be that you talk to him (through prayer) and let him talk to you (through reading the Bible).
2. Grow in the grace and knowledge of Jesus.
3. Renounce ungodly and worldly passions and live upright, self-controlled, and godly lives.
4. Men spoke from God by the Holy Spirit.
5. All scripture is God-breathed (NIV).
6. Teaching, rebuking, correcting, and training in righteousness (NIV)
7. It will help you be approved by God so that you will not be ashamed.

8. The Lord

9. The Lord disciplines us for our good that we might share in his holiness.

10. To go to Nineveh and call out its evil ways

11. Jonah fled to Tarshish.

12. The Lord sent a great wind on the sea, threatening to break up the ship Jonas was on.

13. God told Balaam not to go with those who had come from Moab.

14. God was angry and sent the angel of the Lord to oppose Balaam.

15. Worship God, pray his will be done on earth, pray for your daily necessities, pray for the forgiveness of your sins, pray that you would not be led into temptation, and pray that you would be delivered from evil.

16. Pray in private rather than to be seen by men and be concise in your prayers.

17. (a) Those who persecute you; (b) those who abuse you; (c) all the saints; (d) all people, kings, and all in high positions; (e) yourself.

18. (a) You will receive what you ask for; (b) Jesus will do what you ask for; (c) whatever you ask will be done for you.

19. (a) You don't have because you don't ask; (b) you ask with wrong motives to spend what you get on your pleasures (NIV).

20. We must ask according to God's will.

21. Believe that you have received it.

22. Our iniquities have separated us from God so that he will not hear.

23. Husbands must be considerate of their wives and treat them with respect (NIV).

24. Persevere in prayer without losing heart.

25. First, you would pray in private using few words. You would pray for your daily necessities, the forgiveness of your sins and to be kept from temptation and evil. You would pray for those who persecute or abuse you as well as

all the saints, kings and those in authority, all people and yourself. You would make sure you have removed all hindrances to prayer. And you would pray according to God's will—believing by faith that God will hear and answer everything you have asked that would be according to his will.

26. Devoted themselves to (a) the apostle's teaching, (b) fellowship, (c) breaking of bread, and (d) prayer

27. (a) Do not neglect to meet with other believers and (b) encourage one another.

28. The Father and his son Jesus Christ

29. Christ died for our sins, was buried and rose again on the third day.

30. Repentance toward God and faith in Jesus Christ

31. They should perform deeds in keeping with repentance.

32. For example: you could share that to see or enter the kingdom of God, you must be born again. Then, using John 1:12–13, you could explain that to become a child of God, you must receive Christ and believe in his name. When you do that, you will become a child of God by being born of God—which is a spiritual birth as opposed to a natural one.

Lesson 4

1. That you be conformed to the image of his Son
2. That you be sanctified and be kept blameless at the coming of Christ
3. Positional
4. Progressive
5. The words *might become* indicate progressive.
6. Positional
7. Positional
8. Progressive
9. Positional

10. God will forgive us when we confess our sins, and he will purify us of all unrighteousness.
11. No.
12. He will not allow us to be tempted beyond what we can bear.
13. When he is enticed by his own evil desires (NIV)
14. It leads to sin.
15. Death
16. Our mind should be renewed that we might know the will of God.
17. We destroy arguments and opinions against God and take every thought captive to make it obedient to Christ.
18. He has given us his divine power and precious promises.
19. The Holy Spirit
20. Prayer
21. He has given us new life and delivered us from slavery to sin.
22. The Lord will not listen to our prayers.
23. It is important so that God will forgive your trespasses.
24. Pride would hinder our sanctification because God opposes the proud.
25. Love for the world or the things in the world
26. Friendship with the world shows hatred toward God and makes you an enemy of God.
27. God and we are both responsible for making changes in our life. We work out our salvation, and God works in us both to will and to work for his good pleasure.
28. (a) you are to put off your old self, your old sinful ways; (b) you are to have your mind renewed; (c) you are to put on your new self which is created to be like God in true righteousness and holiness; (d) basically, you are to replace the sinful practice with the godly alternative
29. (a) put away falsehood; b) speak the truth
30. (a) do not steal; (b) work for what you have
31. (a) foul or corrupt language; b) edifying speech

32. (a) bitterness, wrath, anger, clamor, slander and malice; (b) be kind, tenderhearted, and forgiving
33. (a) cast off the works of darkness; b) put on the armor of light
34. (a) put away anger, wrath, malice, slander, obscene talk, and do not lie; b) put on compassionate hearts, kindness, humility, meekness, patience, forgiveness, and love

Lesson 5

1. You should love your neighbor.
2. Love them as you love yourself.
3. You nourish and cherish yourself.
4. We should humbly consider others more significant than ourselves.
5. People will be lovers of self, lovers of money, proud, arrogant, abusive, disobedient to their parents, ungrateful, unholy, heartless, unappeasable, slanderous, without self-control, brutal, not loving good, treacherous, reckless, swollen with conceit, lovers of pleasure rather than lovers of God, having the appearance of godliness, but denying its power.
6. (a) a pharisee and a tax collector; (b) the tax collector; (c) he will be humbled; (d) he will be exalted
7. God opposes them.
8. Grace
9. (a) no one understands or seeks God; (b) all are worthless, not a single one does good; (c) all have sinned (are sinners); (d) of the flesh, sold under sin; (e) hostile to God; (f) they cannot please God
10. (a) they are God's children and will be like him; (b) he is a new creation; (c) we might become the righteousness of God; (d) we are not a slave but one of God's children; (e) we have the Spirit of adoption as sons; (f) we have been set free from sin

11. Rejoice always, pray without ceasing, give thanks in all circumstances.
12. We should be sanctified so that we may become holy.
13. We should be conformed to the image of God's Son.
14. We should offer our bodies as a living sacrifice to God and not be conformed to the world but be transformed by renewing our minds so that we can discern what God's will is.
15. (a) rejoice always in the Lord; (b) let your gentleness be evident to all; (c) do not be anxious about anything; (d) let your requests be made known to God (NIV)
16. A peace that passes all understanding
17. Humble yourself and cast all your anxiety on him.

Lesson 6

1. As a race
2. He is concerned about being disqualified.
3. To know Christ, to know the power of Christ's resurrection, to know the fellowship of sharing in Christ's sufferings, to become like Christ in his death, and to attain to the resurrection from the dead
4. No.
5. He wants to finish the race (NIV).
6. He had finished the race.
7. To see whether you are in the faith
8. Jesus Christ is in you.
9. Jesus Christ is not in you.
10. Death
11. By their works
12. He will also deny them.
13. You are lying and do not practice the truth if you claim to have fellowship with the Lord.
14. They no longer have a sacrifice for their sins and will have a fearful expectation of judgment and of raging fire that will consume the enemies of God (NIV).

15. They are of the devil.

16. Their will is to do the devil's desires who was a murderer from the beginning and does not stand in the truth, because there is no truth in him.

17. They do not make a practice of sinning and cannot keep on sinning.

18. The one who does not practice righteousness or love his brother is not of God but the one who does practice righteousness and love his brother is of God.

19. They will reap destruction.

20. Before

21. Before

22. Before

23. Before

24. Before

25. Before

26. Before

27. Faith required

28. Faith required

29. Faith required

30. Faith required

31. Faith required

32. Faith required

33. Faith required

34. Faith required

35. Faith required

36. By faith

37. First, someone is sent, then he preaches the Word of Christ, then the person hears what is preached, then they believe in Christ and finally call on him and Paul says in Romans 10:13 that those who call on the name of the Lord will be saved.

38. All

39. All

40. All

41. All

42. All
43. All
44. All
45. All
46. All
47. All
48. All
49. Yes.
50. Yes.
51. Yes.
52. Yes.
53. Yes.
54. Yes.
55. Yes.
56. Yes.
57. Cannot be lost
58. Cannot be lost
59. Can be lost
60. Can be lost
61. Cannot be lost
62. Can be lost
63. Can be lost
64. Cannot be lost
65. Can be lost
66. Can be lost
67. Can be lost
68. Cannot be lost
69. Can be lost
70. Can be lost
71. Cannot be lost
72. Cannot be lost
73. Can be lost
74. If you hold fast to the Word I preached to you
75. You are being saved.
76. You believed in vain.

77. If you continue in your faith, established and firm, not moved from the hope held out in the gospel.
78. He (God) has reconciled you by Christ's physical body through death to present you holy in his sight, without blemish and free from accusation.

Lesson 7

1. They are born of God.
2. We are liars if we claim to have fellowship with God but walk in darkness but if we walk in the light we have fellowship with God and Jesus cleanses us from all sin.
3. We know we have come to know Jesus if we obey his commands. We know we are in him if we walk (live) as he did.
4. They will keep (obey) his commands.
5. If you hate your brother, you are walking in darkness, but if you love him, you are in the light.
6. If your works are evil, you love darkness and hate the light, but if you do what is true, you come to the light.
7. If we love our brothers, we have passed from death to life, but hating your brother is equivalent to being a murderer and you have no eternal life in you.
8. Whoever does the will of God
9. If what you heard from the beginning remains in you, then you also will remain in the Son and have eternal life (NIV).
10. No one who abides in Christ keeps on sinning and no one who keeps on sinning has either seen Christ or known him.
11. Whoever makes a practice of sinning is of the devil, but by practicing righteousness and loving your brother, you are of God.
12. We can know we are of the truth by not loving with words or tongue but with actions and in truth (NIV).
13. By loving one another and because God has given us his Spirit
14. Whoever has the Son has life

Harold Bayley is a seventy-year-old retired high school mathematics teacher. He has taught in public, charter, and Christian schools. After suffering a personal tragedy in his early twenties, he turned to the Lord and committed himself to become like Christ. He found from Romans 12 that he had the gift of exhortation. He desires to encourage believers to become like Christ and grow in their faith. Harold grew up in a time without computers. He studied, taught, and memorized scripture. He memorized twelve of the shorter books in the New Testament in perfect word. He does not adhere to any man-made "isms" such as Calvinism, Arminianism, dispensationalism, Pelagianism, etc. As a result, he has a strong desire that believers are sound in doctrine and have the tools and knowledge to overcome sin in their lives. Those are the two main emphases in his work in this book.